THE VEGETARIAN CURRY

In the same series

The Curry Secret
An Indian Housewife's Recipe Book
The Stir Fry Cook

Uniform with this book

THE
VEGETARIAN
CURRY

by

Asha Naran

PAPERFRONTS

Typeset in 10/11pt Times by County Typesetters, Margate, Kent.

Printed and bound in Great Britain by Cox & Wyman Ltd., Reading, Berkshire.

The *Paperfront* series and the *Right Way* series are both published by Elliot Right Way Books, Brighton Road, Lower Kingswood, Tadworth, Surrey, KT20 6TD, U.K.

DEDICATION

TO
ASHOK

without whom none of this
would have been achieved

With acknowledgements to my daughters
Anouska and Sonal (for being willing guinea-pigs)
and my mother who helped with some of the recipes.

CONTENTS

INTRODUCTION

For one reason or another, more and more people are becoming vegetarians. It is more common among the younger generation since older people tend to be less likely to change their habits. I have decided to write this book to help make vegetarianism more exciting for these people, and, believe me, it can be.

Being a vegetarian need not mean surviving on tasteless boiled vegetables, and filling up with fattening cakes and biscuits. It is much more satisfying and interesting to eat tasty wholesome foods. On the other hand, you do not have to be a vegetarian to enjoy the recipes in this book. Even though as a family we eat a lot of vegetarian food, we are by no means committed to vegetarianism. My children are very fond of meat and to them a Sunday without a proper roast lunch would be unthinkable.

The recipes I have included here are generally easy to make. Once you have mastered the basic techniques you will find it simple to produce meals from this book. You will soon learn to cook by 'feel' rather than having to follow a recipe exactly.

Several of the recipes start with the 'popping' of certain spices in hot oil. This technique is called 'Vaghar'. Care should be taken to cover the pan with its lid while the spices are 'popping'. It is safer to take the pan off the heat when adding the vegetables or pulses to the hot oil as it is likely to splatter.

If you wish to invest in some utensils for your Indian cookery I would suggest a heavy based pan, a pressure cooker, a herb mill and a tavi. I find a herb mill very useful for chopping small amounts of adrak (ginger), lasan (garlic) or mircha (green chillies). It also means you can avoid handling the green chillies which cause a burning sensation that can easily be transferred to other parts of the body. If you do have to chop your chillies by hand, make sure you wash your hands properly afterwards. A tavi will be useful if you want to make chapattis, but a non-stick frying pan will do just as well. A tavi is an iron pan which is round and slightly concave. If you are buying one make sure it has a handle! A pair of tongs will also be needed if you are new to chapatti making.

If you are a strict vegetarian you will have to try and balance your diet. In order to do this choose a dish from each of the following sections: Pulses, Vegetables, Rice and/or Bread. Finish your meal with a piece of fresh fruit.

A vegetarian diet is very healthy. It is well known that a large proportion of the British public suffer from constipation. Cancer of the colon is a not uncommon disease in Britain. Even if you are not a vegetarian, changing your diet to include pulses and whole wheat flour can help to prevent these and many other problems.

Indian food need not be hot. It is the unique blend of spices that makes it so palatable. If you do not want your food to be hot, merely reduce the amount of chilli powder. Even though my children love Indian food, they cannot cope with the heat of the chillies. I get round this by serving them first before stirring in chilli powder to the rest of the food in the pan. When they ask for seconds they quite happily settle for the hotter version.

I would also like to point out that 'curry' is a name given to a dish made using haldi (turmeric), chilli powder and other spices. Contrary to popular belief it does not necessarily have to have a thick spicy sauce. You will find several recipes in this book which have hardly any sauce and then there are other recipes which are really quite dry. With dishes like that it is a good idea to serve a raita or a pulse dish.

As far as ingredients go, I have found that most of the ones I have used in this book are very easily found in large supermarkets. Those that are not stocked by them will certainly be found at a reputable Indian grocery shop. Many of the green vegetables will only be found in an Indian shop. For best results vegetables should be cooked when they are still fresh.

As you will notice, I prefer to use teaspoons and tablespoons for measurements. For those who prefer to work in metric, just remember that: 1 teaspoon = 5ml
and 1 tablespoon = 15ml.
Also, the measurement of 'cup' is basically that of an average sized teacup. They are not American cup measures.

I hope this book will open up a whole new world of culinary delights for you.

Bon appétit!

1

SPICES AND INGREDIENTS

Adrak	Ginger	A root which has a very distinctive flavour, ginger is very commonly used in many Asian countries. It is regarded as a warming spice and is therefore used for medicinal purposes as well as for flavouring foods.
Ajma	Carom	Used in foods difficult to digest as it is believed to help digestion.

Amli	Tamarind	A very sour fruit, more commonly available in this country in a block all stuck together. To use, break some off and soak in hot water for 10 minutes, then sieve through a wire mesh, extracting as much juice as possible. This juice is used to give a tangy flavour to some of the dishes.
Dahi	Natural yoghurt	Can be bought but is very easy to make at home (see page 85).
Dhana	Ground coriander	This is one spice that can be used in larger quantities than any other. It has a subtle flavour and is used for thickening sauces.
Dhunia	Green coriander	A green herb very similar to parsley. It is used for garnish in most Indian dishes.
Elchi	Cardamom	Used in many sweet and savoury dishes alike. Whole cardamoms are used in curries while the seeds are crushed and added to sweet dishes. The seeds are also chewed after a meal to aid digestion.
Garam Masala		Literally means 'hot spices'. It is a mixture of several spices in varying proportions. Adds a distinctive Oriental flavour to a dish. For recipe see page 123.

Ghee	Clarified butter	Readily available in most Indian grocery shops but can be made quite easily at home. For instructions see page 84.
Gor	Jaggery	Sugar in the most unrefined state. It is sold in solid blocks and is readily available in most Indian grocery shops. If gor is not available it can be substituted with dark brown sugar.
Haldi	Turmeric	A root similar to ginger. It is yellow in colour and can be used fresh if peeled and minced before use. It is commonly used in powder form and is available in most Indian grocery shops. Haldi is also said to be good for the skin. For a very economical face mask, mix together 1 tablespoon of thick cream, 1 teaspoon of ground haldi and a few drops of lemon juice. Indians who have little money for expensive medicines sometimes rub haldi on cuts as it has antiseptic properties..
Hing	Asafoetida	A strong spice which should be used in small quantities. It is a good digestive aid and is also sometimes mixed to a paste with water and rubbed around the belly button of small babies to help relieve colic.

Jaiphal	Nutmeg	A digestive spice used in many sweet dishes and cordials. Most supermarkets stock nutmeg, either whole or powdered. I think the whole nutmeg has the best flavour and aroma. It can be grated straight into the dish.
Jeera	Cumin	A spice with a wonderful flavour which shows its full potential in yoghurt dishes.
Kala Mari	Black peppercorns	A hot spice widely used in Indian cookery. Used whole in curries it is discarded before serving. Ground peppercorns are used in spicy snacks that are often sold in many Indian grocery shops.
Kessar	Saffron	A very expensive ingredient which must be used in moderation. Mainly used in sweet dishes and biriyanis. It is also sometimes mixed to a paste and rubbed on the foreheads of small babies for relieving colds.
Lasan	Garlic	Strongly flavoured and easily grown in the garden in the summer months. The root is much stronger than the shoots, so when a mild garlic flavour is desired use the top of the plant. Garlic is said to have aphrodisiac properties!
Lavang	Cloves	Widely used in sweet and

		savoury dishes. It has antiseptic properties and is often chewed after meals to freshen the palate.
Limdi	Curry leaves	These grow on bushes and are used for their flavour. Whole leaves are used for garnish and young tender leaves are chosen for chutneys. Fresh leaves are sometimes available in Indian grocery shops but their flavour is nothing like that of freshly picked leaves.
Masala	Spices	A word given to the collective spices used in a dish.
Methi	Fenugreek	A herb with a mildly bitter taste. The seeds produced by the plant have a much stronger bitter taste and are generally used to make pickles and medicinal concoctions.
Mircha	Green chillies	These are very hot and should be used in small quantities. As a rule, the smaller the chilli, the hotter it is. Chillies should be finely chopped or minced before adding to a dish. After handling chillies it is very important to wash hands thoroughly as it is very easy to transfer the heat of the chillies to other parts of the body, such as the eyes. Red chillies can be bought in powder form from most Indian grocery

		shops. Both are used in most Indian dishes and it is this that gives them their distinctive hot flavour.
Rai	Mustard seeds	Used for its pungent flavour, the seed is black and perfectly round. It can also be grown on the kitchen window sill for use in salads.
Tuj	Cinnamon stick	A strong spice used in powdered form in many sweet dishes. The stick cinnamon is more commonly used in curries and is discarded before serving.

2

SUGGESTED MENUS

Below are two examples of how meals are served traditionally in India. Notice that the sweet dish is included in the first course.

Aubergine and Valor Shaak
Bhakhri
Seero
Cucumber Raita

Plain Boiled Rice
Dall

Cauliflower and Pea Shaak
Shrikhand
Puree
Green Coriander Chutney

Plain Boiled Rice
Kadhi

Here I have tried to show how the dishes can be rearranged to suit a Western palate.

Spicy Sweetcorn and Sev

Chick Pea and Potato Curry
Plain Boiled Rice
Puree
Onion Raita

Gulab Jamuns
(served with bought vanilla ice cream)

Tikha Puda

Aubergine Rings
Chapattis
Plain Boiled Rice
Kadhi
Green Coriander Chutney
Tossed Green Salad

Fresh Fruit

Kachori

Undhiu
Matar-Bhaat
Radish Raita

Sev

Bhagia

Masala Dhosa
Sambhar
Spicy Yoghurt Chutney

Basudi with Fruit

Bhagia

Vegetable Curry
Paratha
Cucumber Raita

Gulab Jamuns rolled in coconut

Spicy Sweetcorn with Sev

Special Vegetable Khichri
Kadhi

Fresh Fruit Salad

Vegetable Samosa

Spiced Red Kidney Beans
Layered Chapattis
Plain Boiled Rice
Red Hot Garlic Chutney
Green Salad

Fresh Fruit

Potato Pouwa

Tarka Dall
Jadi Roti
Mixed Vegetable Rice
Green Salad

Basudi with Fruit

3

RICE

In Indian culinary history, rice dates back to as early as 2800 B.C. It is eaten throughout the country and is prepared in various different ways.

Biriyani and pillau must be the two most popular ways of serving rice. While plain boiled rice is perhaps more commonly eaten in most Indian homes, pillaus and biriyanies are usually cooked for special occasions and dinner parties.

Contrary to what most people think, rice is not difficult to cook. First make sure you have a large heavy based pan. Then, if you are making plain rice, make sure you have plenty of water. The exact quantity does not matter as long as the rice can move freely in the boiling water.

To check if rice is cooked, press a grain of rice between

thumb and forefinger. If a hard core is felt then a little more cooking will be required; the grain should feel soft when tested in this way, but do be careful not to over cook the rice. When cooked, strain the rice and return to the pan with some ghee or butter dotted over the surface. Set the pan over a very gentle heat and steam for approximately one minute with the lid tightly closed.

A little more attention will be needed for the other recipes but you will find they are just as simple to cook as long as you follow the recipes correctly. The secret is to use just enough water, or less if you are not sure and then add a little at a time as you go along until it is cooked.

There are various different varieties of rice available on the market. To my mind Basmati rice is perhaps the best one available. It is certainly the best type of rice to eat with Indian food. One exception to this rule is in the preparation of Khichri. I find the American Long Grain rice more suitable for this as it gives a better consistency to the Khichri. Unlike other rice dishes where it is desirable to have each grain of rice separate and fluffy, Khichri should be a stickier mixture. It is an economical dish to prepare and is delicious served with a dollop of ghee and a bowl of hot Kadhi, for both of which you will find recipes in this book (pages 84 and 83).

Rice is also used in the flour form. There are various uses for it in that form. Dhosa is one example. In South India Dhosa and Sambhar is a staple diet. Rice, as we know it, is not normally eaten there. Rice flour is also used in the making of crunchy snacks similar to poppadums. These are usually fried but some varieties can be roasted. These are readily available at most Indian grocery shops.

Now that you have seen how versatile rice can be I hope you will be tempted to try out some of the recipes in this section.

Plain Boiled Rice

This simple rice recipe is very commonly used in everyday cooking. You may use ordinary butter in this recipe if you wish, but in other recipes in this book, where ghee is called for it is important to use it as it will make all the difference to your final dish. For instructions on how to make ghee see page 84. It is also possible to buy ghee from Indian grocery shops.

Serves: 3–4
Preparation time: 15 minutes
Cooking time: 5–7 minutes

225g (½ lb) Basmati rice
1.5 litres (3 pints) water for boiling
1 teaspoon salt
1 tablespoon ghee (see page 84) or butter

Wash the rice in 2–3 changes of water and soak for 15 minutes. Bring water to the boil in a large pan. Strain soaking rice and add to the boiling water. Add the salt, stir and bring back to the boil. Allow to boil for 5–7 minutes or until a grain of rice feels soft when pressed between the thumb and forefinger. Strain the water from the rice and return rice to the pan. Reduce the heat to very low, dot the ghee or butter over the rice, cover and leave for 1 minute.

Matar-Bhaat

This is a delicious alternative to plain boiled rice. The fluffy grains of rice dotted with peas in this recipe look very attractive. This is an ideal dish to serve at a dinner party. In order to keep the grains of rice whole be very gentle when stirring.

Serves: 3–4
Preparation time: 15 minutes
Cooking time: 10–12 minutes

225g (½ lb) Basmati rice
2 tablespoons cooking oil
2 tablespoons ghee (see page 84)
1 teaspoon jeera (cumin)
1 teaspoon rai (mustard seeds)
100g (4 oz) frozen peas (defrosted)
1 teaspoon salt
boiling water for cooking

Wash the rice in 2–3 changes of water and soak for 15 minutes.

In a large heavy based pan, heat the oil and the ghee together. When hot, add the jeera and rai seeds. Allow to 'pop' for a few seconds with the lid on the pan, then add the peas. Cook for 2 minutes over medium heat.

Strain the rice and add to the pan with the salt and stir fry for 2 minutes. Now add boiling water until it covers the rice completely and comes up to approximately 2.5cm (1 inch) above the level of the rice. Cover the pan and cook until the liquid has been absorbed. This should take 5–7 minutes. Test a grain of rice by pressing between the thumb and forefinger. If further cooking is required, sprinkle a little water and cook at very low heat until tender.

Mixed Vegetable Rice

This colourful dish is ideal to serve at dinner parties. Choose a pulse dish and a yoghurt dish to go with it. It is also delicious served cold at picnics. When stirring, take care not to break up the vegetables.

Serves: 6–8
Preparation time: 5–10 minutes
Cooking time: 15–20 minutes

450g (1 lb) Basmati rice
6 tablespoons oil
3 tablespoons ghee (see page 84)
2.5cm (1 inch) tuj (stick cinnamon)
3 lavang (cloves)
2 kala mari (black peppercorns)
1 large onion (chopped)
1 large potato (cubed)
2 carrots (cubed)
125g (4 oz) frozen peas (defrosted)
2 teaspoons salt
1 teaspoon ground haldi (turmeric)
1 teaspoon chilli powder
1 tablespoon dhana (ground coriander)
0.75 litres (1½ pints) boiling water

Wash the rice and soak in warm water. Heat the oil and ghee together in a large pan. When hot, add the tuj, lavang, kala mari and onion and cook for 3 minutes. Add the potato and carrots and cook, covered, over medium heat until tender. Add the peas, salt, haldi, chilli powder, dhana and cook for a further 2 minutes. Drain the rice and add to the pan. Stir fry for 1 minute, reduce the heat, then add the boiling water, cover and cook until all the water is absorbed. Test a grain of rice by pressing between thumb and forefinger. If it is still hard or grainy you will need to add a little more water and cook further until all the water is absorbed and the rice is soft when tested as above.

Khichri

This is a tasty but easy meal to serve. Kadhi and Bhindi Shaak (pages 83 and 53) are the ideal accompaniments. You could, of course, choose any other vegetable dish but Kadhi must always be served with it, along with a dollop of ghee (page 84).

Serves: 6–8
Preparation time: 30 minutes
Cooking time: 10–15 minutes

175g (1 cup) toor dall (split pigeon peas)
350g (2 cups) American Long Grain rice
2 litres (4 pints) water (approximately)
1½ teaspoons salt
½ teaspoon ground haldi (turmeric)
2 cloves lasan, peeled and slivered (garlic)
ghee to serve (page 84)

Soak the toor dall in hot water for half an hour. Wash the rice in 2–3 changes of water and soak for half an hour. In a large heavy based pan bring water to the boil. Wash and drain the toor dall. Also drain the soaking water out of the rice. Add the rice and toor dall to the boiling water in the pan. Bring back to the boil and stir in the salt, haldi and slivered lasan. Boil rapidly until the mixture is cooked. The grains should be quite soft. (Do not worry too much about over cooking this dish.)

Empty into a sieve and drain off all the water left in the pan. Return the Khichri to the pan, lower the heat to very low and simmer with the lid on for one minute.

Special Vegetable Khichri

This wonderful spicy rice is a meal in its own right. It is often served at garden parties and fetes. You could serve it with Kadhi (page 83) or a yoghurt dish if you wished, or perhaps a little mango pickle and poppadums.

Serves: 6–8
Preparation time: 30 minutes
Cooking time: 20–25 minutes

350g (2 cups) American Long Grain rice
2 carrots
1 small potato
½ large onion
½ large aubergine
50g (2 oz) frozen peas
3 cloves lasan (garlic)
2 mircha (green chillies)
4 tablespoons cooking oil
4 tablespoons ghee
2 tuj (sticks of cinnamon)
6 lavang (cloves)
4 elchi (cardamoms)
6 kala mari (black peppercorns)
2 teaspoons salt
1 teaspoon ground haldi (turmeric)
boiling water

Wash the rice in several changes of water and then leave soaking in some fresh water for half an hour.

Meanwhile, peel the carrots and potato and chop finely. Peel and chop the onion finely. Wash and cut the aubergine into 1.5cm (½ inch) cubes. Soak the peas in warm water to defrost. Peel and crush the lasan and chop the mircha very fine.

In a large heavy based pan, heat the oil and ghee

together. Add the tuj, lavang, elchi and kala mari. Throw in the chopped carrots, stir and cover the pan. Reduce the heat to medium and cook for 2 minutes. Add the chopped onion and potato. Stir well and cook, covered, for 3 minutes. Now add the cubed aubergine, salt and haldi. Stir carefully so as not to break up the vegetables and allow to cook for a further 3 minutes with the lid on.

Drain the peas and add to the pan along with the crushed lasan and the finely chopped mircha. Mix well and cook, uncovered, for 1 minute.

Add the drained rice and stir fry gently for 2 minutes. It is very important to stir gently at this stage as the soaked rice will break easily. Now add enough boiling water to cover and rise to about 2.5cm (1 inch) above the contents of the pan.

Cover tightly and simmer gently for the next 10 minutes. Stir occasionally until the rice is cooked and all the water is absorbed. Add a little more hot water if the contents of the pan seem to be going too dry.

4

PULSES

In India a large percentage of the population is vegetarian. They rely mainly on pulses for their protein. Pulses are very versatile and are used in a variety of ways in all parts of India. Some pulses are difficult to digest and in such cases the combination of spices used helps to overcome this problem.

The word 'dall' is used to describe the form of the pulses used. Dall is merely the split form, so for example, split moong would be moong dall, etc. You will see from the recipes that follow in this section that the dalls require a much shorter cooking time.

Before cooking pulses and dalls it is necessary to check to see if there are any small stones or discoloured pulses which should be discarded before commencing to wash and cook them. Do this by taking the amount to be cleaned on a tray or a large plate and, starting with the pile at one side of the tray, bring a little at a time to the middle. Spread out the small amount of grains and remove any impurities, then gather the cleaned grains and push these to the other end of the tray. Repeat in this way until you have sifted through all the grains you will be using.

I have included several recipes in this section for you to try. For some of these recipes a pressure cooker would be very useful but if you do not have one it is possible to cook the pulses in an ordinary pan. Boil rapidly in plenty of water for 10 minutes, then reduce heat and simmer until the pulses are quite soft. This may take up to 2½ hours. Check from time to time to see if more water is required in the pan. Always add only boiling water to maintain the simmering point. It is best to use all the cooking liquid in the final dish, and just keep boiling to evaporate any excess liquid until the dish reaches the consistency desired.

Chana	Chick peas	These are rich in iron and there are several ways of cooking them. It is usually necessary to soak them overnight. A pressure cooker is very useful when cooking whole pulses. Flour made from chick peas is often called gram flour or besan. It forms the basis of many Indian snacks.
Masoor	Whole lentils	These are flat and round in shape. They are often found in biriyani dishes, soups and stuffings. They have a high food value as they are rich in protein.

Moong	Mung beans	These small, green beans are very popular. All Indian homes would have them. They are an excellent stand-by in the store cupboard. They can also be sprouted for use in salads.
Toor	Pigeon peas	These can be cooked whole but would require overnight soaking. Split pigeon peas, more commonly known as toor dall, are used to make dalls and sambhars. It is very easy to mistake split chick peas (chana dall) for split pigeon peas (toor dall). The toor dall is oily in appearance and slightly bigger than chana dall.
Urid	Black beans	Whole urid are black but they are rarely used whole, more commonly being de-husked and split or ground into flour. In the presence of water, urid flour becomes very sticky and it is this characteristic which makes it ideal for making poppadums.

Spiced Red Kidney Beans

This is a firm favourite with my family. As it is quite a substantial dish I serve it simply with chapattis (page 64) or, for a quicker meal, plain boiled rice (page 23). I have even served it with baked potatoes on Bonfire Night. It went down a treat!

If you are short of time or prefer not to use dried beans which need careful soaking and rapid boiling, a 425g

(15 oz) can of red kidney beans from the supermarket may be used instead, but omit the salt in the recipe and only add it at the end if needed. It is a good idea to keep a can in the store cupboard for those unexpected guests.

Serves: 4–6
Preparation time: overnight
Cooking time: 25–35 minutes
Special equipment: pressure cooker

225g (8 oz) red kidney beans (soaked overnight)
1.14 litres (2 pints) water
3 tablespoons cooking oil
1 teaspoon ajma seeds (carom)
1 large onion, chopped
1½ teaspoons salt
1 teaspoon chilli powder
1 teaspoon ground haldi (turmeric)
3 tablespoons dhana (ground coriander)
1 medium sized can tomatoes, chopped (400g)
2 cloves lasan, crushed (garlic)
2 teaspoons granulated sugar
1 tablespoon chopped dhunia (green coriander) to garnish

Rinse the soaked kidney beans and place in a pressure cooker with the water. Cook for 15 minutes at high pressure setting. Kidney beans must be cooked properly in this way otherwise they are poisonous. Beans should remain whole but be easily squashed between thumb and forefinger.

Heat the oil in a heavy based pan, add the ajma seeds and let them sizzle for a few seconds before adding the chopped onion. Cook for 2 minutes. Add the salt, chilli powder, haldi and dhana. Stir fry for 1 minute, add tomatoes, lasan and sugar.

Simmer for 5 minutes then add the cooked beans with all the cooking liquid (or, if using canned beans, the complete contents of the can, including the liquid) and simmer for 15 minutes.

Moong Curry

This dish can be served quite thick with chapattis (see page 64) or watery like soup with fresh bread and butter. It is equally delicious served cold with a swirl of yoghurt on a hot summer's day. Moong is high in protein and fibre which makes it an ideal dish for someone on a diet.

Serves: 6–8
Preparation time: 5 minutes
Cooking time: 1 hour 20 minutes

450g (1 lb) moong (mung beans)
1.75 litres (3½ pints) boiling water
1 medium sized can tomatoes (400g)
2 mircha (green chillies)
2.5cm (1 inch) adrak, peeled (root ginger)
3 tablespoons cooking oil
1 teaspoon rai (mustard seeds)
3 teaspoons jeera seeds (cumin)
2 teaspoons salt
1 teaspoon chilli powder
1 teaspoon ground haldi (turmeric)
2 tablespoons dhana (ground coriander)
2 tablespoons gor (jaggery) or brown sugar
juice of 1 lemon
1 tablespoon chopped dhunia (green coriander) for garnish

Wash the moong and add to boiling water in a pan. Boil for 1 hour, adding more boiling water during cooking time if necessary.

Mince together the tomatoes, mircha and adrak. Heat the oil in a heavy based pan, add the rai and jeera seeds and cover the pan for a few seconds until the 'popping' stops. Add the tomato mixture and bring to the boil. Simmer, covered, for 2 minutes.

Add the salt, chilli powder, haldi, dhana, gor or brown sugar, and the lemon juice. Mix well and simmer for another 2 minutes.

Add the moong with all the water it has been cooking in, stir and simmer for 15 minutes.

Chick Pea and Potato Curry

This is a very good dish to serve at a dinner party as it can be cooked in advance and re-heated just before serving. In fact, I find it tastes much better the day after when the chick peas have had time to absorb all the spices. Serve with fulecha for a buffet party or on a bed of plain boiled rice for a wholesome evening meal (see pages 72 and 23).

Serves: 6–8
Preparation time: overnight
Cooking time: 20–30 minutes
Special equipment: pressure cooker

225g (½ lb) chana (chick peas)
1 litre (2 pints) water
2 large potatoes – not peeled
4 tablespoons cooking oil
1 teaspoon rai (mustard seeds)
1 teaspoon jeera seeds (cumin)
¼ teaspoon hing powder (asafoetida)
1 large onion (chopped)
3 cloves lasan, peeled (garlic)
2.5cm (1 inch) adrak, peeled (root ginger)
1½ teaspoons salt

1 teaspoon chilli powder
3 tablespoons dhana (ground coriander)
2 teaspoons ground haldi (turmeric)
2 teaspoons sugar
1 tablespoon sesame seeds
1 medium can tomatoes, chopped (400g)
juice of 1 lemon
2 tablespoons chopped dhunia (green coriander)

Soak the chana overnight. Wash and place in a pressure cooker with 1 litre (2 pints) of water and cook at high pressure for approximately 20 minutes, or until tender. Meanwhile, boil the potatoes in a separate pan until just cooked. Remove from the water and allow to cool completely. Peel and cut into 2.5cm (1 inch) cubes. (Leaving the skins on ensures they don't break up in cooking.)

Heat the oil in a large pan. When hot, add the rai and jeera seeds, cover, and allow to 'pop' for a few seconds. Then add the hing and quickly throw in the chopped onion. Stir, and cook, covered, for 3 minutes, or until lightly browned. Stir occasionally. Mince the lasan and adrak and add to the pan. Stir fry for approximately 30 seconds then add the salt, chilli powder, dhana, haldi, sugar and sesame seeds. Stir fry for 1 minute and add the chopped tomatoes.

Bring to the boil and simmer for 5 minutes. Then add the cubed potatoes, cooked chana with 300ml (½ pint) of the cooking liquid and the lemon juice. Stir well, bring to the boil and simmer for 5 minutes.

If a thicker curry is wanted, boil rapidly with the lid off until the desired consistency is reached.

Serve garnished with chopped dhunia.

Tarka Dall

The mixture of the three dalls gives this dish an unusual taste and texture. It should have a thick porridge-like consistency and I like to serve it with purees and Mixed Vegetable Rice (see pages 71 and 24).

Serves: 6–8
Preparation time: 30 minutes
Cooking time: 40 minutes
Special equipment: pressure cooker

145ml (½ cup) moong dall (split mung beans)
145ml (½ cup) chana dall (split chick peas)
145ml (½ cup) toor dall (split pigeon peas)
1 tablespoon urid dall (split black beans)
1 litre (2 pints) boiling water
3 tablespoons cooking oil
1 teaspoon rai (mustard seeds)
1 teaspoon jeera seeds (cumin)
¼ teaspoon hing powder (asafoetida)
2 tablespoons dhunia (green coriander) chopped
2 teaspoons salt
1 teaspoon ground haldi (turmeric)
1 teaspoon chilli powder
2 tablespoons dhana (ground coriander)
1 small can chopped tomatoes (230g)
2.5cm (1 inch) adrak, peeled and grated (root ginger)
2 tablespoons gor (jaggery) or brown sugar
2 mircha (green chillies)

Mix together the moong dall, chana dall and toor dall and soak in warm water for half an hour. Soak the urid dall separately. Wash the mixed dalls and place in a pressure cooker with 2 pints of boiling water. Pressure cook for 30 minutes at a low setting. The dalls should now be mushy. Wash and drain the urid dall.

Heat the oil in a heavy bottomed pan. When hot, add the rai and jeera seeds, cover and allow to 'pop' for a few seconds before adding the hing and the urid dall, but take care as this will splatter. Reduce the heat, add the chopped dhunia and stir fry for 1 minute.

Now add the salt, haldi, chilli powder and dhana and stir fry for another minute. Stir in the chopped tomatoes and grated adrak. Bring to the boil and simmer for 5 minutes. Add the gor or brown sugar. Slit the mircha lengthwise and add to the tomato mixture, remembering to wash your hands thoroughly after handling them. Lastly, add the cooked dall mixture. Boil away until thick and soupy.

Chana Dall

(split chick pea curry)

With its thick, orange flavoured sauce, this dish makes a wonderful evening meal. It is also high in protein. Serve it with layered chapattis (page 67), plain boiled rice (page 23) and some green salad or, for a dinner party, with other vegetable dishes.

Serves: 4
Preparation time: 30 minutes
Cooking time: 15–20 minutes

225g (½ lb) chana dall (split chick peas)
500ml (1 pint) warm water
3 cloves lasan, peeled (garlic)
3 mircha (green chillies)
6 tablespoons cooking oil
1 teaspoon rai (mustard seeds)
1 teaspoon jeera seeds (cumin)
¼ teaspoon hing powder (asafoetida)
1 teaspoon ground haldi (turmeric)

(contd. overleaf)

Chana Dall (contd.)

1½ teaspoons salt
500ml (1 pint) hot water
juice of 1 orange
2 tablespoons chopped dhunia (green coriander) for garnish

Soak the chana dall in the warm water for half an hour. Wash it in several changes of water and drain. Mince the lasan and mircha together and keep aside. (Don't forget to wash your hands after handling the mircha.)

Heat the oil in a heavy based pan. Add the rai and jeera seeds and allow to 'pop' for a few seconds with the lid on. Add the hing and the drained chana dall and quickly cover the pan to avoid the oil from splattering. After about 10 seconds, uncover the pan and add the haldi, salt and the minced lasan and mircha and mix well. Cook for 1 minute, stirring continuously, then add the hot water. Bring to the boil, cover and cook for 15 minutes or until the chana dall is tender. Stir occasionally during this time and add more hot water if required. Lastly, stir in the orange juice and simmer for 1 minute. Empty into a serving dish and sprinkle with the chopped dhunia.

Vall Ki Dall

(split white beans)

This dish is very popular with the older generation as vall has a slightly bitter taste. Because of this it is served with Kadhi (see page 83) which is tangy and so compensates for the bitter taste of the vall. This dish should have a thick porridge-like consistency. The ajma seeds are used in this recipe to aid digestion as beans can be hard to digest.

Serves: 4–6
Preparation time: 5 minutes
Cooking time: 45 minutes
Special equipment: pressure cooker

450g (1 lb) vall (white beans)
1 litre (2 pints) boiling water
5 tablespoons cooking oil
1 teaspoon ajma seeds (carom)
1½ teaspoons salt
1 teaspoon ground haldi (turmeric)
1 teaspoon granulated sugar
5 mircha (green chillies)
2 cloves lasan, peeled (garlic)
150ml (5 fl. oz) dahi (natural yoghurt)

Wash the vall and put in a pressure cooker with the water and cook for 30–40 minutes at medium pressure setting. For this recipe the vall should be very well cooked, almost mushy.

In another pan heat the oil and add the ajma seeds. Very carefully add the vall with all the cooking water. Add the salt, haldi, sugar, mircha and lasan and cook, stirring, for 5 minutes.

Add the dahi and blend well. Simmer with the lid off until the mixture is thick.

Moong Dall

When cooked, this dish has a soft consistency rather like paté. I like to serve it for the first course at dinner parties with toast triangles or with toasted pitta bread which I buy from a supermarket. For best results, brush a little hot water on both sides of a pitta bread and toast under a hot grill until golden. Butter the hot pitta bread and cut into wide strips. Serve with Moong Dall and a wedge of lemon. Alternatively, as a light supper dish, serve with chapattis (page 64).

Serves: 4–6
Preparation time: 5 minutes
Cooking time: 25 minutes

225g (½ lb) moong dall (split mung beans)
2 cloves lasan (garlic)
2 mircha (green chillies)
3 tablespoons oil
1 teaspoon rai (mustard seeds)
1 teaspoon salt
1 teaspoon ground haldi (turmeric)
750ml (1½ pints) boiling water
lemon wedges to serve

Wash and drain the dall. Mince the lasan and mircha together. (Remember to wash your hands after handling mircha.)

Heat the oil in a pan, add the rai and cover until they have stopped 'popping'. Add the dall with the lasan and mircha. Stir fry for 1 minute, then add the salt and haldi. Mix well.

Add the boiling water and simmer until most of the water has been absorbed. Test the dall between the thumb and forefinger. If more cooking is required, add a cupful of boiling water. Test again when liquid has been absorbed.

Dall

(split pigeon pea soup)

The population of the state of Gujarat in India is essentially vegetarian. This dish, when served with plain boiled rice, a vegetable and a yoghurt dish, provides the protein in this typical Gujarati meal.

Serves: 6
Preparation time: 10 minutes
Cooking time: 1 hour 20 minutes

125g (4 oz) toor dall (split pigeon peas)
1.5 litres (3 pints) boiling water
1 teaspoon methi seeds (fenugreek)
1 mircha (green chilli)
2 tablespoons gor (jaggery) or brown sugar
1 medium size can of tomatoes (400g)
2.5cm (1 inch) adrak (root ginger)
2 tablespoons oil
1 whole dry red chilli
1 teaspoon rai (mustard seeds)
1 teaspoon jeera seeds (cumin)
1 pinch hing powder (asafoetida)
2 teaspoons salt
1½ teaspoons chilli powder
1 teaspoon ground haldi (turmeric)
2 tablespoons dhana (ground coriander)
juice of 1 lemon
3 tablespoons chopped dhunia (green coriander) for serving

Soak the toor dall in a little boiling water for 10 minutes. Wash, drain and bring to the boil in a heavy based pan with 1.5 litres (3 pints) water and the methi seeds.

Cook for about 1 hour or until the toor dall is cooked and mushy. Whisk thoroughly and continue to simmer gently.

Split the mircha lengthwise and add to the pan with the gor or sugar. (Wash your hands thoroughly after handling mircha.) Mince the tomatoes and adrak.

In another pan heat the oil, add the whole dry red chilli, then add the rai and jeera seeds, cover and allow to 'pop'. Remove from heat and just before adding the tomatoes and adrak, throw in a pinch of hing. Bring to the boil, add the salt, chilli powder, haldi, dhana and simmer for 5 minutes.

Add the tomato mixture to the toor dall and simmer for another 10 minutes. Add lemon juice and adjust seasoning as required. Sprinkle with chopped dhunia before serving.

Dall Dhokri

(split pigeon pea soup with dumplings)

This is a delicious all-in-one dish. It can be served for lunch or for supper, on its own or accompanied with a salad. It is also a very good way of using up any left over Dall (above).

Serves: 4
Preparation time: 10–15 minutes
Cooking time: 30 minutes (plus 1 hour 20 minutes for cooking the Dall)

Follow the previous recipe for Dall, then make the Dhokri as follows:

2.5cm (1 inch) tuj (cinnamon stick)
5 lavang (cloves)

Dhokri
100g (4 oz) gram flour (ground chick peas)
25g (1 oz) juwar flour (ground barley)

25g (1 oz) chapatti flour (ground wheat)
½ teaspoon salt
½ teaspoon red chilli powder
1 clove lasan, crushed (garlic)
0.5cm (¼ inch) adrak, finely chopped (root ginger)
¼ teaspoon ground haldi (turmeric)
2 teaspoons dhana (ground coriander)
pinch hing powder (asafoetida)
3 tablespoons oil
water
oil and lemon juice to garnish

Bring the Dall to the boil. Add the tuj and lavang and allow to simmer while you make the Dhokri.

Mix all the ingredients together and add enough water to make a stiff dough. Divide the dough into tangerine sized balls and roll out one ball at a time on a floured board. Cut into diamond shapes and gently lower a few at a time into the bubbling Dall. Allow the Dall to reach boiling point between each addition of Dhokri. Simmer, uncovered, for 30 minutes.

To serve, dish out into individual soup plates, pour 2 tablespoons of oil over it and a squeeze of lemon.

Vaddu

This dish has a special significance in the Hindu religion. Once a year women gather to pray for healthy babies and these prayer meetings always end with a communal meal of Vaddu and Rotla, an unleavened bread. At other times chapattis are served with this dish (page 64). (Rotla is regarded as poor men's bread and so it is not used in everyday cooking.)

Serves: 4–6
Preparation time: 2 days
Cooking time: 15 minutes
Special equipment: pressure cooker

285ml (1 cup) moong (mung beans)
145ml (½ cup) masoor (whole lentils)
warm water
5 tablespoons cooking oil
1 teaspoon rai (mustard seeds)
1 teaspoon jeera seeds (cumin)
4 mircha, minced (green chillies)
2.5cm (1 inch) adrak, minced (root ginger)
2 cloves lasan, minced (garlic)
2 teaspoons salt
1 teaspoon ground haldi (turmeric)
1 pint hot water

Combine the moong and masoor and soak overnight in warm water. Drain and tie loosely in a warm, damp cloth and leave in a warm place for 2 days, but check twice a day to make sure the cloth does not dry out completely. By the end of two days the moong should have grown quite long roots.

Wash and drain the (germinated) vegetable mixture. In a pressure cooker, heat the oil and add the rai and jeera seeds and cover with the lid. Wait until they have stopped 'popping', then add the moong mixture and cook for a minute, stirring. Reduce the heat, add the minced mircha, adrak and lasan. Also add the salt and haldi and cook for a further minute. (Remember to wash your hands thoroughly after handling mircha.)

Add the hot water, stir and close the lid of the pressure cooker and cook under low pressure for about 10 minutes. If a lot of liquid remains, reduce down by boiling rapidly with the lid off.

Mori Dall

(plain dall)

This simple pigeon pea dish is well worth trying. Spoon some onto a plate of plain boiled rice (see page 23), add a dollop of ghee (page 84) and serve this with a bowl of hot Kadhi (page 83). It is quite delicious. It is also a very nutritious and economical meal which is very easy to make.

Serves: 4
Preparation time: 15–20 minutes
Cooking time: 15–20 minutes

100g (4 oz) toor dall (split pigeon peas)
500ml (1 pint) boiling water
½ teaspoon salt
½ teaspoon ground haldi (turmeric)

Soak the toor dall in 250ml (½ pint) of the boiling water. Leave to soak for 15–20 minutes. Wash the toor dall in several changes of water and drain. Put the rest of the boiling water in a pan with the toor dall and bring back to the boil. Add the salt and the haldi and simmer gently with the lid partly closed and cook for 15–20 minutes or until the toor dall is soft and pulpy.

This dish should not be runny. If there seems to be too much liquid in the pan continue simmering with the lid off until a thick mushy mixture is left.

5

VEGETABLES

In the Gujarat state of India most of the inhabitants are vegetarian, and therefore vegetables play an important part in their diets. Over the years they have devised hundreds of ways of cooking them, some with no sauce at all, some with just a hint of sauce and some in which the vegetables are literally swimming in a thick aromatic sauce.

Follow the recipes in this section and you will see that eating vegetables need never be boring again. I hope that when you become confident with the techniques of cooking vegetables the Indian way, you will try to make up your own dishes with vegetables of your choice.

When choosing vegetables make sure you buy only the freshest. They have the best flavour. They are also easier to cook and when some of the recipes in this section call for little or no water, this will depend on how fresh the vegetables are.

For a balanced vegetarian meal you should serve a vegetable dish, a pulse dish, a bread or rice dish and a yoghurt dish. Refer to the suggested menus at the front of the book to see how this is done. Of course, it may not be possible to cook three or four different dishes and in that case I suggest you have a pulse dish with a rice or bread dish. This combination is nutritious as well as filling.

The **aubergine** *is a very versatile vegetable. I am always tempted to buy them when I see fresh looking ones in the shops. They are now stocked in most supermarkets and are usually quite reasonably priced.*

Aubergine and Potato Curry

The dark skin of the aubergine contrasts very well with the potato in this dish and I would serve it at a dinner party with purees, Mixed Vegetable Rice and Tarka Dall (see pages 71, 24 and 36). More simply, you could serve it with plain rice or chapattis (pages 23 and 64).

Serves: 4–6
Preparation time: 5 minutes
Cooking time: 20–25 minutes

1 large aubergine
6 small potatoes, peeled
4 tablespoons cooking oil
1 teaspoon rai (mustard seeds)
1 teaspoon jeera seeds (cumin)
1½ teaspoons salt
½ teaspoon ground haldi (turmeric)

(contd. overleaf)

Aubergine and Potato Curry (contd.)

1 teaspoon chilli powder
2 tablespoons dhana (ground coriander)
½ cup water – if necessary
1 small can tinned tomatoes (230g)

Wash and cut the aubergine into large chunks and halve the potatoes. Heat the oil in a heavy based pan, add the rai and jeera seeds and cover for a few seconds until the 'popping' has stopped. Add the aubergine, salt and haldi. Mix well, reduce heat and cook, covered, for 2 minutes.

Add the potatoes, chilli powder and dhana, stir and cook, covered, for 15 minutes or until the vegetables are tender. Add ½ cup of water if required, but if the aubergine is fresh it should not be necessary to add any water.

Chop the tomatoes and add to the pan. Cook for another 5 minutes.

Variation: substitute 225g (½ lb) frozen peas for the potatoes.

Aubergine and Valor Shaak

Valor is a type of bean. I have only ever found them at Indian grocery shops. Do make sure that they are fresh as this dish is cooked with little or no water and when the vegetables are fresh they give out their own juices. If the heat is kept very low, these juices are usually enough to cook the dish.

Serve on a freshly made paratha, topped with Cucumber Raita (pages 69 and 82), or with rice or chapattis (pages 23 and 64).

Serves: 4
Preparation time: 5 minutes
Cooking time: 45 minutes

450g (1 lb) green valor beans (available at most Indian grocers)
1 large aubergine
5 tablespoons cooking oil
1 teaspoon rai (mustard seeds)
1 teaspoon jeera seeds (cumin)
1 teaspoon ground haldi (turmeric)
1½ teaspoons salt
1½ teaspoons chilli powder
2 tablespoons dhana (ground coriander)
1 teaspoon granulated sugar
water
3 tomatoes

Wash the valor beans and prepare by snapping off the tips and pulling off strings along both sides of the bean. Pull the beans open and cut in half lengthwise. Wash the aubergine and cut into large chunks.

Heat the oil in a heavy based pan, add the rai and jeera seeds. Cover the pan for a few seconds until the seeds have all 'popped'. Add the drained aubergine and valor beans, mix with a wooden spoon, add the haldi and salt and cook, covered, over very low heat for 10 minutes.

Add the chilli powder, dhana, sugar and a sprinkling of water if required. Continue cooking over low heat until the vegetables are tender (about 30 minutes).

Chop the tomatoes and spread over the vegetables and cook for a further 5 minutes. Stir very carefully and serve.

Aubergine Rings

This can be served as a side dish at a dinner party. Prepared in advance it can then be kept warm in an oven or be re-heated in a microwave oven just before serving. The stacks of vegetables (layers of aubergines and potatoes) in this recipe should be kept intact during cooking.

Serve with freshly made chapattis or rice (pages 64 and 23) and Kadhi (page 83).

Serves: 4–6
Preparation time: 5–7 minutes
Cooking time: 10–15 minutes

1 teaspoon salt
1 teaspoon ground haldi (turmeric)
1½ teaspoons chilli powder
3 tablespoons dhana (ground coriander)
2 tablespoons gram flour (ground chick peas)
2 teaspoons granulated sugar
8 tablespoons cooking oil
1 large aubergine
water
1 large potato
3 tablespoons dahi (natural yoghurt)

In a small bowl put the salt, haldi, chilli powder, dhana, gram flour, sugar and 3 tablespoons of the oil. Mix to a smooth paste.

Wash and slice the aubergine into thick rings and keep immersed in water to prevent discolouration of the flesh. Peel and slice the potato into thick rings.

Take the remainder of the oil in a large frying pan. Drain the aubergine and potato slices and spread out on a board. Rub the masala paste on one side of all the slices. Make up piles of vegetables in the frying pan with the masala side up, in alternate layers, starting with aubergine slices.

Cook, covered, over very low heat until the vegetables are tender. Spoon the dahi over all the vegetable piles and gently turn each pile over. Cook with the lid off for 2 minutes and serve.

Bhindi *or* **okra** *is also sometimes known as Ladies Fingers because of its long slender appearance. It is now available from most large supermarkets. I prefer to cook this vegetable without water as I find water makes it sticky and unappetising. The lid should be left off the pan during most of the cooking time to avoid condensation falling back into the pan causing the contents to go sticky. It should be cooked until tender and slightly crisp.*

Bhindi Masaledar

(okra in a sauce)

In this recipe I add some dahi (natural yoghurt) in the last 5 minutes to make a tangy sauce. Serve this dish with plain boiled rice (see page 23).

Serves: 3–4
Preparation time: 5–7 minutes
Cooking time: approx. 40 minutes

450g (1 lb) bhindi (okra)
5 tablespoons cooking oil
1 teaspoon jeera seeds (cumin)
1 teaspoon salt
1 teaspoon ground haldi (turmeric)
1½ teaspoons chilli powder
400ml (¾ pint) dahi (natural yoghurt)

Wash the bhindi and allow to dry on a clean tea towel. Top and tail, then slice into 1cm (¼ inch) thick rings.

Heat the oil in a heavy pan, add the jeera seeds and sizzle, covered, for a few seconds. Add the prepared bhindi, salt and haldi and toss. Cover and cook for 5 minutes over medium heat. Stir, add the chilli powder and reduce heat. Cook without the lid for 30 minutes, or until the bhindi is tender and not so sticky.

Add yoghurt, bring to the boil and simmer for 5 minutes. Taste and add more salt and chilli powder if needed.

Bhinda Ravaya

(stuffed okra)

As this dish has no sauce of its own, it is usually served with Kadhi and plain boiled rice (see pages 83 and 23). For a dinner party you may wish to serve it alongside a yoghurt dish, such as Cucumber Raita (page 82).

Serves: 3–4
Preparation time: 10 minutes
Cooking time: 10 minutes

450g (1 lb) bhindi (okra)
1 teaspoon salt
1 teaspoon chilli powder
1 teaspoon ground haldi (turmeric)
4 tablespoons dhana (ground coriander)
8 tablespoons cooking oil

Wash bhindi and spread on a clean tea towel to dry. Top and tail, then split lengthwise on one side only.

Mix the salt and all the spices together in a bowl using 4 tablespoons of the oil to make masala stuffing and use it to stuff the bhindi lightly.

Heat the remaining oil in a frying pan and add the prepared bhindi. Lower the heat and cook, covered, until tender. Remove the lid, turn the heat up slightly and cook, stirring, until crisp on the outside.

Bhindi Shaak

This dish is served with plain rice, Kadhi and chapattis (pages 23, 83 and 64) for a main meal. To serve it for a light supper, simply roll it in chapattis and top with Cucumber Raita (page 82).

Serves: 2–3
Preparation time: 5 minutes
Cooking time: 15–20 minutes

450g (1 lb) bhindi (okra)
4 tablespoons cooking oil
1 teaspoon methi seeds (fenugreek)
1 teaspoon salt
1 teaspoon ground haldi (turmeric)
1 teaspoon chilli powder
1 tablespoon dhana (ground coraind er)
1 teaspoon granulated sugar

Wash the bhindi and spread out on a clean tea towel to dry. Top and tail, then slice into thick rings. Heat the oil in a frying pan and sizzle the methi seeds in the hot oil for a few seconds.

Add the bhindi, salt, haldi, chilli powder, dhana, and sugar. Mix well and cook, covered, for 2 minutes.

Lower the heat to medium and cook, uncovered, for 15 minutes or until tender and not sticky. Stir occasionally during cooking time.

Cabbage and Carrot Stir Fry

This is a side dish that can be prepared in just a few minutes. Serve it instead of a salad when accompanied by a dish from the pulses section of this book. Alternatively, rolled up in a chapatti it makes a quick and easy lunch.

Serves: 4–6
Preparation time: 5 minutes
Cooking time: 2–3 minutes

225g (½ lb) carrots
225g (½ lb) white cabbage
3 mircha (green chillies)
6 tablespoons cooking oil
2 teaspoons rai (mustard seeds)
¼ teaspoon hing powder (asafoetida) – optional
1 teaspoon salt

Peel and grate the carrots thickly. Shred the cabbage finely. Split each one of the mircha lengthwise into four (and wash hands thoroughly after handling them).

Heat the oil in a wok or a large frying pan. Add the rai, cover, and allow to 'pop' for a few seconds. Add the hing and then immediately throw in the rest of the ingredients. Stir fry for a minute or two, according to preference. The vegetables should be crisp and crunchy.

Cauliflower and Pea Shaak

This is a spicy vegetable dish that can be served as a side dish at a dinner party. (The word 'shaak' means it is a vegetable dish with little or no sauce.) I like to serve it for supper rolled up in freshly made chapattis (see page 64), with a squeeze of lemon.

Serves: 3–4
Preparation time: 2–5 minutes
Cooking time: 10–15 minutes

6 tablespoons cooking oil
1 teaspoon rai (mustard seeds)
1 teaspoon jeera seeds (cumin)
1 medium cauliflower, divided into florets
1½ teaspoons salt
1 teaspoon ground haldi (turmeric)
225g (½ lb) frozen peas
1½ teaspoons chilli powder
2 tablespoons dhana (ground coriander)
½ teaspoon garam masala to serve

Heat the oil in a large heavy pan. Add the rai and jeera seeds and cover pan for a few seconds until the 'popping' stops.

Add the cauliflower, salt and haldi and toss to cover the florets with oil.

Add the peas, chilli powder and dhana. Toss again to coat evenly.

Turn the heat down to low, cover tightly and cook until the cauliflower is tender.

Sprinkle with garam masala (see page 123) and serve.

Vegetable Curry

Vegetable curry is ideal to serve at a dinner party. Either serve it with plain paratha (see page 69), or with Matar-Bhaat (page 23). Green Coriander and Coconut Chutney (page 77) goes very well with it. You could also buy a jar of mango pickles, available from Indian grocery shops, for a final touch.

Serves: 4
Preparation time: 5 minutes
Cooking time: 35–40 minutes

5 tablespoons cooking oil
2 lavang (cloves)
2.5cm (1 inch) tuj (cinnamon stick)
3 kala mari (black peppercorns)
1 large onion, chopped
1 medium can tomatoes (400g)
2 tablespoons tomato purée
1½ teaspoons salt
1 teaspoon ground haldi (turmeric)
2 tablespoons dhana (ground coriander)
1 teaspoon chilli powder
1 large potato
2 medium sized carrots
1½ cups hot water
125g (4 oz) frozen peas

Heat the oil in a heavy based pan, add the lavang, tuj, kala mari and onion and cook for 5 minutes.

Chop or liquidize the tomatoes and add to the pan. Cook for a further 2 minutes. Add the tomato purée, salt, haldi, dhana and chilli powder and cook for 3 minutes.

Cut the potato and carrots into large chunks and add to the pan. Cook, covered, for 5 minutes over medium heat.

Add the water and cook for 15 minutes. Add the peas

towards the last 5 minutes of cooking time.

Variation: Hard boil 4 eggs, and at the end of the cooking as above, cut them into two, lengthwise, and add to the curry. Sprinkle with garam masala and mix gently, being careful not to break up the vegetables.

Green Bean Shaak

Any variety of green beans can be used for this dish but the best ones are the stringless varieties. Frozen green beans can also be used for this recipe but add 150ml (¼ pint) of water with the salt, chilli powder, haldi, etc. and cook very slowly until tender. Serve this dish with freshly made chapattis (page 64).

Serves: 4–6
Preparation time: 5 minutes
Cooking time: 15–20 minutes

450g (1 lb) stringless green beans
1 large onion
3 tablespoons cooking oil
1 teaspoon ajma seeds (carom)
1 teaspoon salt
1 teaspoon chilli powder
1 teaspoon ground haldi (turmeric)
1 tablespoon dhana (ground coriander)
1 small can tomatoes (230g)

Top and tail beans and wash thoroughly. Slice thinly lengthwise and cut into 5cm (2 inch) pieces. Slice the onion.

Heat the oil, add ajma seeds and after they have sizzled, add the prepared beans and onion. Add the salt, chilli powder, haldi, dhana and mix well.

Reduce the heat and cook, covered, for 10 minutes or until the beans are tender. Chop the tomatoes, add to the beans and cook for another 5 minutes.

Mixed Vegetable Curry

This is a good supper dish. Serve it on a bed of plain boiled rice or with plain parathas (see pages 23 and 69). Care should be taken when stirring as the vegetables break up easily and you will be left with a pot of mush!

Serves: 6–8
Preparation time: 5 minutes
Cooking time: 25 minutes

6 tablespoons cooking oil
2.5cm (1 inch) tuj (cinnamon stick)
3 lavang (cloves)
2 kala mari (black peppercorns)
2 elchi pods (cardamom)
1 large onion (sliced)
2 cloves lasan, crushed (garlic)
5 small potatoes, peeled and halved
3 carrots, peeled and cut into 2.5cm/1 inch squares
2 teaspoons salt
1 teaspoon ground haldi (turmeric)
½ cauliflower, divided into florets
1 green pepper, deseeded and cut into 2.5cm (1 inch) squares
2 teaspoons chilli powder
2 tablespoons dhana (ground coriander)
1 teaspoon granulated sugar
1 cup water
1 medium can tomatoes (400g)
3 tablespoons tomato purée
125g (4 oz) frozen peas
½ teaspoon garam masala

Heat the oil in a heavy pan and add the tuj, lavang, kala mari, elchi pods, onion and garlic. Stir fry for 1 minute, then add the potatoes, carrots, salt and haldi and mix well.

Reduce the heat, cover and cook for 10 minutes, stirring occasionally. Add the cauliflower, green pepper, chilli powder, dhana, sugar and water and cook, covered, for 5 minutes.

Add the tomatoes, tomato purée and peas and cook for another 10 minutes. If there is excess liquid left in the pan, boil away with lid off until the sauce is quite thick and coats the vegetables in the pan.

Sprinkle with garam masala and serve hot.

Potato Shaak

This is a favourite dish with my family. I suppose the best way to describe it is to liken it to chips. Spicy chips! I like to serve it with plain boiled rice, Dall and some freshly made chapattis (see pages 23, 41 and 64) for a dinner party. Include a yoghurt dish and some mango pickles to complete the meal. A large variety of ready made pickles are available from Indian grocery shops.

Serves: 4–6
Preparation time: 5 minutes
Cooking time: 10–15 minutes

8 tablespoons oil
1 teaspoon rai (mustard seeds)
1 teaspoon jeera seeds (cumin)
450g (1 lb) potatoes, peeled, halved and sliced
1½ teaspoons salt
1 teaspoon ground haldi (turmeric)
1 teaspoon chilli powder
1 tablespoon dhana (ground coriander)
1 teaspoon granulated sugar
1 tablespoon dhunia (green coriander)

Heat the oil in a large frying pan, add rai and jeera seeds and close the lid until the 'popping' stops.

Add the potato slices, salt, haldi and mix well. Reduce heat, add the chilli powder, dhana and sugar, mix to coat all the potato slices, cover and cook for 5–7 minutes or until the potatoes are cooked.

Remove the lid, turn up the heat and cook, stirring gently, until crisp and lightly browned.

Garnish with dhunia.

Whole Onion Shaak

It is surprising how this, one of the more common vegetables, is changed into an exotic dish by the use of a few spices. This is one of my favourite dishes and I like to serve it simply with freshly made chapattis (see page 64). It may also be served with parathas or rice (pages 69 and 23).

Serves: 4
Preparation time: 10–15 minutes
Cooking time: 30 minutes

450g (1 lb) shallots or small onions, peeled
1cm (½ inch) adrak (root ginger)
1 teaspoon salt
1 teaspoon chilli powder
1 teaspoon ground haldi (turmeric)
3 tablespoons dhana (ground coriander)
2 tablespoons chopped dhunia (green coriander)
1 teaspoon granulated sugar
8 tablespoons oil
water

Cut each shallot into four segments lengthwise, cutting only three quarters of the way down so that the segments are held together.

Mince the adrak finely and add to the salt, chilli powder, haldi, dhana, dhunia, sugar and 2 tablespoons of the oil. Mix well to create masala filling and use it to fill the shallots.

In a heavy pan, heat the remainder of the oil and add the prepared shallots. Turn the heat down to minimum and cook, covered, until the shallots are tender. Stir frequently and if the masala begins to stick to the bottom of the pan add a little water, about 2 tablespoons at a time.

Undhiu
(mixed vegetables)

This is an all-in-one dish. The principle is similar to the French dish ratatouille. All the vegetables are put into a large pot along with all the spices and seasonings and are cooked slowly in their own juices. Serve with chapattis and raita (pages 64 and 82).

Serves: 4
Preparation time: 10 minutes
Cooking time: 20–25 minutes

1 medium aubergine
6 small new potatoes
125g (4 oz) mange tout peas
125g (4 oz) frozen peas
2.5cm (1 inch) adrak (root ginger)
25g (1 oz) raw peanuts
1 teaspoon salt
1 teaspoon ground haldi (turmeric)
1½ teaspoons chilli powder
3 tablespoons dhana (ground coriander)
2 tablespoons chopped dhunia (green coriander)
1 teaspoon granulated sugar
8 tablespoons oil

Wash and cut the aubergine into fairly large chunks. Scrape and halve potatoes and top and tail mange tout peas.

Mince the adrak and peanuts together. Add the salt, haldi, chilli powder, dhana, dhunia, sugar and oil. Mix well to form masala paste. Add to the vegetables and stir to coat all the pieces evenly.

Place in a heavy based pan and cook, covered, until the vegetables are tender. Keep heat to the minimum throughout cooking time.

6

INDIAN BREADS

Indian breads consist of Chapatti (Roti), Paratha, Puree, Bhakhri, etc. They are basically unleavened breads. Unlike other breads you do not require the use of an oven to cook these. They can be cooked on a tavi or a griddle or even a frying pan.

Rolling a chapatti is probably the first thing an Indian mother teaches her young daughter. The child is often given a piece of dough to practise on while mother makes her daily batch of chapattis.

Puree is a fried bread and is therefore only made for special occasions. Unlike the paratha and chapatti, puree is served with both sweet and savoury dishes. By adding a few spices to the mixture before binding the ingredients into a dough, puree can also be served as a snack. It is therefore very versatile.

A bhakhri is similar to a chapatti but it is rolled much thicker and cooked with a little oil on the tavi or frying pan. It should be lightly browned and crisp on the outside and yet soft inside. To munch a freshly cooked bhakhri is truly a mouth-watering experience.

In this section I have included recipes for a variety of Indian breads. You will find that they make all the difference to your meal. An Indian housewife would never dream of serving her curries with anything but some freshly cooked Indian bread of one sort or another. I do hope you will try making some. They are not difficult once you get the hang of them.

Chapatti

(roti)

Of all the breads, I think chapattis are those eaten most often. They can be served with most curries and they are especially good with the shaak dishes (see pages 48 – 60). As they are rolled thinly and roasted, rather than fried, they are lighter and easier to digest. If you are new to chapatti making I suggest you use tongs to turn your chapattis over when cooking them on the wire rack, which should be set over very high heat. Both gas and electric cookers are suitable for making chapattis.

Serves: 4–6
Preparation time: 10–15 minutes
Cooking time: 1–2 minutes

450g (2 cups) chapatti flour (ground wheat)
2 tablespoons oil
hot water

ghee (page 84) for spreading
plain flour for rolling

Put the chapatti flour into a bowl, add the oil and mix lightly. Add enough hot water to form a soft dough. If the dough is sticky, add a teaspoon of melted ghee to the bowl and continue to knead.

Divide the dough into walnut sized pieces. Set your griddle on a medium setting. If you don't have a griddle, then a heavy frying pan or a tavi will do. You will also need a wire rack set on an open flame or a very hot radiant ring.

Flatten a piece of dough between the palms of your hands and dip it in the plain flour. Now roll out to a thin round chapatti, approximately 15cm (6 inches) in diameter.

Cook for 1 minute on the griddle (or frying pan), turning once. Do not add any oil or butter to the frying pan as chapattis are cooked dry.

Turn onto the wire rack over high heat. The chapatti should, at this stage, bubble up into a round balloon. Turn quickly to avoid burning. When lightly browned on both sides, put on a warm plate and spread with ghee. Pile the chapattis on top of each other as you make them. Do not worry if your chapattis won't bubble up completely. They will be quite acceptable if you cook them on both sides without burning them.

Jadi Roti
(thick chapatti)

These are very simple to make and are good to serve with curries and pulses. Serve them hot or cold or pack them for a picnic with Moong Dall (page 39) and a salad.

Serves: 4–6
Preparation time: 10–15 minutes
Cooking time: 10–15 minutes

450g (1 lb) chapatti flour (ground wheat)
1 teaspoon salt
3 tablespoons cooking oil
hot water
3–4 tablespoons melted ghee (page 84)
plain flour for dusting

Put the chapatti flour and salt into a large bowl, add the oil and rub in. Add enough hot water to form a soft, pliable dough. Divide the dough into large tangerine sized balls.

Heat a tavi or a non-stick frying pan over medium heat. Also set a wire rack over high heat. (If you are using gas you can turn it up and down when required.) Flatten each ball between the palms of your hands, coat in plain flour and roll out to a 5cm (2 inch) disc. Brush with a little melted ghee. Sprinkle on some plain flour and bring up the edges to enclose the ghee and plain flour and form back into a ball. Flatten again between your palms and roll out on a floured board to 15cm (6 inches) in diameter.

Cook on a heated tavi or frying pan for 1 minute, turning once after 20–30 seconds. Turn onto the wire rack over high heat and cook, turning quickly until bubbled up and lightly browned. Repeat this process with the rest of the balls. Brush melted ghee over each roti (chapatti) as it cooks and stack them up.

Layered Chapattis

(or rotis)

These are ideal to serve with curries and pulse dishes, and can be presented hot or cold, either on the side or with the curry or pulse dish spooned over it. In this way they can be served as a first course or a main course.

Serves: 6
Preparation time: 30–35 minutes
Cooking time: 2–3 minutes each

450g (1 lb) chapatti flour (ground wheat)
1 teaspoon salt
2 tablespoons cooking oil
hot water
2–3 tablespoons melted ghee for brushing (page 84)
plain flour for dusting

Put the chapatti flour and the salt in a large bowl, add the oil and rub in with the fingertips. Add enough hot water to form a pliable dough. Divide the dough into large tangerine sized balls. Roll each ball out on a floured board to about 15cm (6 inches) in diameter. *Brush melted ghee over the round shape and dust with a little plain flour. Fold in half and repeat twice from *. You should end with a rough triangular shape. Do the same with the rest of the balls.

Now heat a tavi or a non-stick frying pan over a low to medium heat. Carefully flatten each layered piece of dough on a floured board to approximately 5mm (¼ inch) in thickness. Try and keep the basic shape triangular as you roll out. Cook each chapatti slowly on the tavi or frying pan, turning frequently, until it has bubbled up and is marked with golden spots all over. Brush a little ghee on the cooked chapatti and cool on a wire rack. Make all the chapattis in this way.

Bhakhri

(shallow fried bread)

A freshly cooked bhakri is quite delicious eaten on its own. It is often served with Dall (see page 41). Unlike chapattis, you do not stack bhakhris. They should be spread out on a wire rack to cool. This helps to keep them crisp until you are ready to serve. In an Indian home, bhakhris are sometimes served instead of chapattis when entertaining guests.

Serves: 6–8
Preparation time: 10–20 minutes
Cooking time: approx. 2 minutes each

6 tablespoons melted ghee (page 84)
450g (2 cups) chapatti flour (ground wheat)
warm water
oil for frying

Rub the ghee into the flour, then use enough warm water to make a firm dough. Divide the dough into walnut sized pieces.

Heat a heavy frying pan or tavi over a medium heat. Roll out bhakhri (the dough), thick and small – approximately 7cm (3 inches) in diameter. Cook on both sides in the frying pan without oil. Then add a teaspoon of oil and allow bhakhri to bubble up. Turn and cook the other side. Bhakhris should be golden brown and crisp on the outside.

Variation: To make sweet bhakhri, dissolve 4 tablespoons of sugar in the water which is added to make the dough.

Plain Paratha

This bread is thick and round and quite substantial so allow one or two per person, according to their appetite. Serve these with any of the shaak dishes (pages 48 – 60) and Spicy Yoghurt Chutney (see page 79) for a delicious main course at a dinner party. They are also good with curries.

Serves: 4–6
Preparation time: 20–30 minutes
Cooking time: 3–4 minutes each

3 tablespoons oil
450g (2 cups) chapatti flour (ground wheat)
1 tablespoon dahi (natural yoghurt)
warm water
125g (4 oz) plain flour (for dipping, sprinkling and rolling)
slightly salted butter, softened

Mix the oil into the flour. Make a hole in the middle, add the dahi and enough warm water to make a soft dough.

Divide the dough into small tangerine sized pieces, flatten each piece between the palms of your hands and dip in flour. Roll out one at a time into a round circle. Spread lightly with softened butter and sprinkle with plain flour. Fold in half and repeat the process. Fold into a quarter and spread again. Sprinkle plain flour on the quartered piece and gather up the three corners and roll lightly between the palms to a flattened ball.

Roll out on a floured board into a thick round shape – approximately 12cm (5 inches) in diameter. Cook slowly on the griddle or a heavy frying pan over a medium heat. Turn several times until the paratha is lightly browned on both sides.

Stuffed Paratha

There are several variations of this dish and once you have mastered the basic principle you will be able to experiment with many different fillings of your choice. When rolling out each paratha handle very gently to avoid having the filling ooze out. Serve hot with a pulse dish and Spicy Yoghurt Chutney (page 79) or with one of the yoghurt dishes.

Serves: 4–6
Preparation time: 30 minutes
Cooking time: 2–3 minutes each

225g (½ lb) chapatti flour (ground wheat)
2 tablespoons oil
warm water
3 mircha (green chillies)
2.5cm (1 inch) adrak (root ginger)
½ bunch dhunia (green coriander)
2 large potatoes, boiled and mashed
1 teaspoon salt
1 teaspoon ground haldi (turmeric)
1 tablespoon sesame seeds
2 tablespoons desiccated coconut
1 teaspoon granulated sugar
oil for shallow frying

Combine the flour, oil and enough warm water to form a soft dough.

Mince the mircha and adrak and chop the dhunia finely. Mix with the remaining ingredients and form into walnut sized stuffing balls. (Remember to wash your hands thoroughly after handling mircha.)

Divide the dough into slightly larger balls. Make a hole in the middle of a ball of dough and place a ball of stuffing in it and bring the dough over the top to cover the stuffing.

Seal well and roll out on a lightly floured board into a flat round shape, approximately 12cm (5 inches) in diameter.

Set a heavy based frying pan over medium heat and shallow fry the parathas using 1 tablespoon of oil at a time. Turn the parathas and cook the other side. They should be crisp and golden on the outside.

Puree

(fried round bread)

When purees are served to guests they inevitably feel special. The reason for this is the time and patience it takes to roll out each individual puree to a perfect round. They are very versatile as they can be served with any of the vegetable dishes in this book and are often served with Shrikhand (see page 109) as a sweet dish.

Serves: 6–8
Preparation time: 25–30 minutes
Cooking time: 10–15 seconds per batch

340g (1½ cups) chapatti flour (ground wheat)
50g (¼ cup) ghee, melted (page 84)
warm water
oil for deep frying

Rub the flour and ghee together. Add enough warm water to make a soft dough.

Divide the dough into small brazil nut sized pieces. Flatten each piece between the palms and roll out on a floured board to small, fairly thin round shapes. Spread out on a clean tea-towel.

Deep fry immediately in hot oil, turning once. The purees would normally blow up into a ball as soon as they are put into hot oil, but if they don't, just fry them until they are lightly brown on both sides.

Fulecha
(fried bread)

This is ideal to serve at buffet parties. Make a day in advance and store in an airtight container to keep them soft. Serve a variety of different vegetable and pulse dishes (see pages 31 – 62) which the guests can spoon over their fulecha. They're also good to serve with a curry.

Serves: 6–8
Preparation time: 20 minutes
Cooking time: 5–10 minutes

450g (2 cups) chapatti flour (ground wheat)
3 tablespoons oil
1 teaspoon salt
2 tablespoons dahi (natural yoghurt)
hot water
oil for deep frying

Use the above ingredients to form a soft dough and divide into four equal parts.

Roll out on a lightly floured board to about 3mm (⅛ inch) thickness.

Cut into large diamond shapes and deep fry in hot oil until puffed up and lightly browned (approximately 1 minute for each batch).

7

PICKLES, CHUTNEYS AND RAITAS

These are essential to a meal, especially if the meal is very plain or mild. Chutneys and pickles help tantalize our taste buds and add a certain 'je ne sais quoi' to the meal. Raitas (yoghurt-based sauces), on the other hand, add a tang to the meal and some of them actually help to cool down a hot curry. The idea is to choose the appropriate pickle or raita for each meal.

Most of the dishes in this section can be put together in a matter of minutes. The hotter, more concentrated chutney should be eaten in very small quantities. It is normally served on the side of the plate and is dipped into now and again or is mixed into just a small amount of the food at a time. If you handle mircha (chillies), don't forget to wash your hands thoroughly afterwards.

Pickled Green Pepper

This pickle is usually served with plain boiled rice and Kadhi (see pages 23 and 83). Include a vegetable dish of your choice and Mori Dall (page 44). This will keep well in a refrigerator for up to 2 days.

Preparation time: 2 minutes
Cooking time: 10–15 minutes

250g (½ lb) green peppers
8 tablespoons cooking oil
1 teaspoon rai (mustard seeds)
¼ teaspoon hing powder (asafoetida)
½–1 teaspoon salt
1 teaspoon ground haldi (turmeric)
2 tablespoons dhana (ground coriander)
½ teaspoon chilli powder
3 tablespoons gram flour (ground chick peas)

Wash and cut the peppers into 2.5cm (1 inch) squares. Heat the oil in a non-stick frying pan, add the rai and cover for a few seconds. Wait until the 'popping' has stopped then add the hing powder to the oil and throw in the green peppers.

Reduce heat to low, add the salt and haldi and stir the contents of the frying pan. Cover and cook at low heat for 10 minutes stirring occasionally. If the peppers start to stick to the bottom of the pan, add 2 tablespoons of water. Continue cooking until the peppers are tender.

Add the dhana and chilli powder and mix well. Sprinkle the gram flour over the peppers and cook, covered, for 1 minute. Stir and cook, uncovered, for a further 2 minutes.

Remove from heat and allow to cool. Refrigerate when cold and use within 2 days.

Pickled Mircha
(pickled chillies – very hot)

These pickles are readily available at Indian Grocery shops but I like to make them as I usually have a lot of home-grown mircha in the garden during the summer months. The rai dall (split mustard seeds) can also be obtained from Indian Grocery shops. For best results use only fresh mircha.

Preparation time: approx. 2½ hours
Cooking time: nil

450g (1 lb) mircha (green chillies) – the long and thin variety
1½ tablespoons coarse salt
1 tablespoon methi seeds, crushed (fenugreek)
100g (4 oz) rai dall (split mustard seeds)
1 teaspoon hing powder (asafoetida)
2 teaspoons ground haldi (turmeric)
140ml (½ cup) oil
1 teaspoon rai (mustard seeds)
juice of 8 fresh lemons

Wash and de-stalk the mircha, cut into 2.5cm (1 inch) pieces and split in half lengthwise. Mix the salt into the mircha and set aside for about 2 hours, or until some liquid is seen in the bottom of the bowl. (Remember to wash your hands thoroughly after handling mircha.)

Roast and crush methi seeds. In a bowl, mix together the rai dall, hing powder, haldi and the crushed methi seeds. Add to the mircha.

Heat the oil in a small pan, add the rai and cover with

lid until the 'popping' stops. Pour over the chilli mixture immediately.

Heat the lemon juice up to boiling point and allow to cool completely. Pour over the chilli mixture and mix thoroughly.

Bottle in clean sterile bottles (wash and dry off in the oven for 10 minutes at 400F/200C/Gas mark 6) and store. Ready to eat after 2 weeks.

Coconut and Garlic Chutney

This chutney will keep well in a refrigerator for up to a week. Serve with any of the pulse dishes in this book. Use sparingly as this is quite a hot chutney.

Preparation time: 5–10 minutes
Cooking time: nil
Special equipment: liquidizer

100g (4 oz) fresh coconut
100g (4 oz) lasan (garlic)
2.5cm (1 inch) adrak (root ginger)
6 mircha (green chillies)
½ teaspoon salt
juice of 1 lemon

Grate the coconut and peel the lasan. Chop up the adrak and mircha into small pieces. (Wash hands thoroughly after handling mircha.)

Put all the ingredients in a liquidizer and liquidize until smooth, or grind together into a smooth paste.

Keeps, refrigerated, for up to 1 week.

Green Coriander and Coconut Chutney

This is another yoghurt dish to serve with curries or pulses. As it is quite hot I would serve it with a mild curry. It can also be served with bhagias or samosas (pages 91 and 98).

Preparation time: 5–7 minutes
Cooking time: nil

1 bunch dhunia (green coriander)
½ fresh coconut
4 mircha (green chillies)
1cm (½ inch) adrak (root ginger)
1 teaspoon jeera seeds (cumin)
500ml (1 pint) dahi (natural yoghurt)
1½ teaspoons salt

Wash and chop the dhunia finely. Grate the coconut, mince the mircha and adrak together and coarsely grind the jeera seeds. (Wash hands thoroughly after handling the mircha.)

Combine all the ingredients together and mix thoroughly until quite smooth.

Keeps, refrigerated, for up to 1 week.

Red Hot Garlic Chutney

This chutney can be served with any Indian meal. It is extremely hot and only half a teaspoonful is placed on the side of the plate to be incorporated into the meal a little at a time. Serve it with mild or medium curries to give people a chance to choose the degree of hotness they desire.

Preparation time: 5–7 minutes
Cooking time: nil

15 cloves lasan (garlic)
2 tablespoons chilli powder
½ teaspoon salt
1 tablespoon oil

Peel and crush the garlic. Work the chilli powder into the garlic. Add the salt and oil and mix to a smooth paste.

Keeps well for several weeks in a refrigerator.

Tomato Chutney

This chutney is served with a variety of snacks. Try it with bhagias or samosas (pages 91 and 98).

Preparation time: 5 minutes
Cooking time: 5–7 minutes
Special equipment: liquidizer

2 large ripe tomatoes
1 large potato
2 tablespoons ghee (see page 84)
1 teaspoon salt
4 mircha (green chillies)
10–12 limdi (curry leaves) – optional

Skin the tomatoes by putting them into hot water for 1 minute and then into cold water for 1 minute. The skins should then peel off with very little effort.

Grate the potato and rinse in fresh water. Heat the ghee in a frying pan and cook the grated and drained potato until tender, stirring continuously. Allow to cool.

Add to the rest of the ingredients and liquidize. (Remember to wash hands after handling mircha.) Bottle and store in the refrigerator. Can be kept for up to 1 week.

Spicy Yoghurt Chutney

This is very quick and easy to put together and is ideal to serve with most curries. It is especially good served with Idli or Masala Dhosa (see pages 104 and 102). To make dahi (natural yoghurt) at home see page 85.

Preparation time: 5–10 minutes
Cooking time: nil

500ml (1 pint) dahi (natural yoghurt)
2 mircha (green chillies)
1 bunch dhunia (green coriander)
2 cloves lasan (garlic)
1½ teaspoons salt
2 teaspoons freshly ground jeera seeds (cumin)

Put the dahi in a bowl and beat until smooth. Mince together the mircha, dhunia and the lasan and add to the yoghurt. (Remember to wash your hands after handling mircha.) Add the salt and freshly ground jeera seeds and mix well.

Taste and adjust the seasoning if necessary.

Keeps, refrigerated, for up to 1 week.

Green Mango Chutney

This delicious tangy chutney is ideal to serve with pulse dishes. I like to serve it with plain boiled rice, Dall and a vegetable dish (see pages 23 and 41). It also goes well with Moong Dall or Chana Dall (pages 39 and 37). Green mangoes are seasonal and are only available in this country during the spring and early summer months. You will find them at Indian grocery shops.

Preparation time: 5–10 minutes
Cooking time: nil
Special equipment: liquidizer

225g (8 oz) green mango flesh, peeled
1 large onion
6 mircha (green chillies)
2 cloves lasan (garlic)
2 teaspoons jeera seeds (cumin)
1 teaspoon salt

Roughly chop the peeled mango flesh and the peeled onion. Put the mango and the onion in the container of a liquidizer along with the rest of the ingredients. Liquidize until quite fine. Empty into a glass bowl and adjust seasoning if required.

Will keep well in a refrigerator for up to 1 week.

Green Coriander Chutney

The dhunia (green coriander) in this recipe should be rinsed in several changes of water to get rid of any soil still stuck to the leaves and stems. Serve it with Kadhi (page 83) and a vegetable or pulse dish. This is a hot chutney, so use it sparingly. Mix a little at a time into your food according to taste.

Preparation time: 5–7 minutes
Cooking time: nil

1 bunch dhunia (green coriander)
6 mircha (green chillies)
2 cloves lasan (garlic)
2 teaspoons jeera seeds (cumin)
½ teaspoon salt
juice of 1 lemon
1 tablespoon oil

Mince the dhunia, mircha and garlic. Crush the jeera seeds and add to the chilli mixture with the salt, lemon juice and oil. Mix thoroughly and use sparingly as it is very hot. (Remember to wash hands after handling mircha.)

Keeps well, if refrigerated, for up to 1 week.

Sev and Yoghurt Chutney

Sev is a crispy spaghetti-like snack made from gram flour (ground chick peas). It is usually served sprinkled over another more substantial snack. An example of this is Spicy Sweetcorn (page 93). There are shops which specialize in Indian snacks like Sev, but if you feel adventurous you could try making your own (see page 94).

Preparation time: 3–5 minutes
Cooking time: nil
Special equipment: liquidizer

500ml (1 pint) dahi (natural yoghurt)
50g (½ cup) sev
3 mircha (green chillies)
2 teaspoons jeera seeds (cumin)
1½ teaspoons salt
½ bunch dhunia (green coriander)

Liquidize everything together. Quick and easy and goes well with most curries.

Keeps, refrigerated, for up to 1 week.

Onion Raita

This is a perfect accompaniment to a hot curry as it helps to cool it down. Try serving it with Vegetable Curry or Green Bean Shaak (see pages 56 and 57).

Preparation time: 5–10 minutes
Cooking time: nil

1 large onion (chopped)
500ml (1 pint) dahi (natural yoghurt)
1½ teaspoons salt
2 teaspoons crushed jeera seeds (cumin)
1 teaspoon powdered mustard

Mix all the ingredients thoroughly until smooth.
Keeps, refrigerated, for up to 1 week.

Cucumber Raita

This goes especially well with vegetable dishes. It is also the usual accompaniment to Dall (page 41).

Preparation time: 5–7 minutes
Cooking time: nil

1 cucumber
500ml (1 pint) dahi (natural yoghurt)
1½ teaspoons salt
2 teaspoons crushed jeera seeds (cumin)

Grate the cucumber and squeeze out most of the liquid. Combine all the ingredients and mix thoroughly until smooth.
Keeps, refrigerated, for up to 1 week.

Radish Raita

This can be served as an accompaniment to vegetable dishes or as a dip at parties. Use crisps and savoury biscuits for dipping or try Fulecha to go with it (see page 72).

Preparation time: 3–5 minutes
Cooking time: nil

50g (2 oz) radish
2 mircha (green chillies)
2 teaspoons crushed jeera seeds (cumin)
1½ teaspoons salt
1 tablespoon chopped dhunia (green coriander)
500ml (1 pint) dahi (natural yoghurt) (page 85)

Grate the radish, reserving 1 for garnish. Chop the mircha finely (and remember to wash your hands thoroughly after handling them).

Combine the grated radish, chopped mircha, crushed jeera seeds, salt and the chopped dhunia in a bowl.

Add the dahi and mix until smooth. Empty into a glass serving bowl and decorate with slices of the reserved radish.

Keeps, refrigerated, for up to 1 week.

Kadhi

(hot yoghurt soup)

Like Dall, Kadhi also originates from the state of Gujarat. When serving Kadhi it is necessary to include a pulse dish in the meal to provide the protein. If a vegetable dish is also being served then plain Dall (page 41) will be sufficient.

Preparation time: 7–10 minutes
Cooking time: 3–5 minutes

500ml (1 pint) dahi (natural yoghurt)
300ml (½ pint) water
2 tablespoons gram flour (ground chick peas)
2 mircha (green chillies)
1cm (½ inch) adrak (root ginger)
1½ teaspoons jeera seeds (cumin)
1 teaspoon salt
1 teaspoon granulated sugar
1 tablespoon ghee
5 limdi (curry leaves)
1 tablespoon chopped dhunia (green coriander)

Put the dahi and water in a bowl, add the gram flour and whisk vigorously for 1 minute. Mince the mircha and adrak and add to the bowl (remembering to wash your hands after handling mircha). Crush one teaspoon of the jeera seeds and add to the bowl with the salt and sugar. Mix well together, taste and adjust seasoning as required.

Heat the ghee in a small pan, add the remaining jeera and sizzle for a few seconds. Remove from heat, add the limdi and pour into the dahi mixture. Add the dhunia and leave in a cool place until ready to serve.

To serve, bring Kadhi up to the boil, stirring continuously, and serve immediately.

Ghee
(clarified butter)

Ghee is simple to make but it is very important to watch it all the time. It can quite easily boil over so make sure you have a large pan. A heavy based pan is preferable as it allows more even distribution of heat. I have suggested a quantity of butter, but you may wish to make more or less. It is entirely up to you.

Preparation time: nil
Cooking time: 10 minutes

450g (1 lb) butter

Place the good quality butter in a large, heavy based pan. Heat thc pan gently until all the butter has melted. Continue to simmer the melted butter until it is clear and glass-like. If it threatens to boil over take it off the heat immediately and stir continuously until the froth subsides. Put the pan back on low heat and continue to stir until the melted butter is clear.

When this stage is reached, take the pan off the heat and stand for 2 minutes. This will allow the residue to sink to the bottom of the pan. Now, very gently, strain into a glass or enamel container with a lid to separate the clear ghee from the residue. Take care not to disturb the sediment which must be discarded.

The ghee will become firm as it cools. Keep in a cool place and use as required. If made properly it should last for 2 months or more.

Dahi
(natural yoghurt)

I find this the easiest thing in the world to make, hence I never buy it at a supermarket. The only requirement is a good, thick tea cosy, large enough to go over the container you are using to set the dahi in. Do give it a try. You will never buy your yoghurt from a supermarket again!

Preparation time: nil
Cooking time: 1 hour
plus, leave to stand overnight

1 litre (2 pints) milk, semi-skimmed or full fat
2 tablespoons dahi (natural yoghurt)

Bring the milk to the boil and simmer for 5 minutes. Pour the milk into the container you have decided to make the dahi in. Glass or enamel containers are best for this purpose. Allow to cool for 40–50 minutes, until tepid. To test the temperature, dip a clean finger in the milk. It should be just bearable. Now take 3 tablespoons of the warm milk and stir into the dahi until smooth. Add this mixture to the warm milk and give it a good stir.

Cover the container and slip a tea cosy over it. Leave overnight and you should have some lovely firm dahi in the morning.

Refrigerate and use within 3 days. Remember to save 2 tablespoons of dahi to use as culture to make your next lot.

8

SNACKS AND SAVOURIES

Indians are great ones for snacks. Young and old alike, all enjoy munching on spicy savouries between meals.

There is no limit to the variety of snacks and savouries in Indian cuisine. Apart from the dry ones such as Sev, Ghathia and Chevda, which can be bought at specialised shops or at Indian grocery shops, there are also many more substantial snacks. Sometimes two of these different types of snack are served together. There are recipes for both kinds of snack in this chapter, including one for Sev although a special utensil is required in the making of Sev, so you may prefer to buy it ready made.

Samosas are probably the best known Indian savoury in

the Western world. They can be bought ready made but I have included a recipe for you to try. Contrary to popular belief, samosas are not difficult to make.

Many of these snack dishes may be used as starters at dinner parties. More substantial dishes like Idli or Masala Dhosa can even be served as the main course.

Potato Pouwa

(spiced potato and flaked rice)

This is a snack made from potato and flaked rice. It can be served almost any time of day. Some people have it for breakfast, some have it at tea time and some even have it as a light lunch or supper. It is an ideal dish to make when unexpected guests arrive.

Serves: 4
Preparation time: 5–10 minutes
Cooking time: 15–20 minutes

450g (1 lb) potatoes
6 tablespoons cooking oil
1 teaspoon rai (mustard seeds)
1 teaspoon jeera seeds (cumin)
2 teaspoons salt
2 teaspoons ground haldi (turmeric)
125g (¼ lb) pouwa (flaked rice)
5 mircha (green chillies)
3 cloves lasan (garlic)
1 tablespoon sesame seeds
juice of 1 lemon
2 tablespoons chopped dhunia (green coriander)

Peel the potatoes and cut into 2.5cm (1 inch) cubes. Heat the oil in a large frying pan. When hot, add the rai and jeera seeds, cover and allow to 'pop' for a few seconds. Then add the potato cubes to the pan taking great care as this will make the oil splatter.

Add the salt and haldi, stir, cover and reduce the heat to medium. Cook, covered, until the potato cubes are just tender. Stir several times during cooking.

In the meantime, rinse the pouwa with warm water and drain. Mince the mircha and lasan and add to the potato in the pan. Sprinkle the sesame seeds and stir well. (If you've handled the mircha, make sure you wash your hands well.) Cook with the lid off for 1 minute, then add the drained pouwa and mix well. Cover and cook for 2 minutes over very gentle heat. Add the lemon juice and chopped dhunia and mix everything once again. Adjust the salt if necessary.

Tikha Puda

(spicy pancakes)

These are usually served as a snack with a cup of tea. Eat them as they are or spread a tablespoon of honey over them for a sweet and spicy taste. You could also serve them for the first course at a dinner party, in which case serve with Spicy Yoghurt Chutney (see page 79) to pour over the Puda. Left over Puda mixture can be refrigerated. Use within two days.

Serves: 8–10
Preparation time: 10 minutes plus 6 hours proving time
Cooking time: 2 minutes each

450g (2 cups) gram flour (ground chick peas)
225g (1 cup) coarse cornflour
60g (¼ cup) whole wheat flour

(contd. overleaf)

Tikha Puda (contd.)

2.5cm (1 inch) adrak (root ginger)
4 mircha (green chillies)
3 cloves lasan (garlic)
2 teaspoons salt
1 teaspoon ground haldi (turmeric)
1 tablespoon dhana (ground coriander)
1 teaspoon granulated sugar
5 tablespoons dahi (natural yoghurt)
6 tablespoons cooking oil
warm water
either: **1 bunch green methi (fenugreek)**
or: **1 grated green paw paw**
or: **1 large, finely chopped onion**
oil for cooking

In a large bowl, combine all the ingredients (except your chosen vegetable) and enough warm water to make a batter consistency. Leave in a warm place for at least 6 hours. Remember to wash your hands after handling mircha.

When you are ready to make the Puda, mix into your batter one of the vegetables suggested.

Heat a tavi or a frying pan on medium heat. Brush about a teaspoon of oil over it and pour a ladleful of batter into the tavi. Spread the batter with the back of a spoon into a round shape. Cover and leave for 1 minute. Using a flat object like a spatula, gently ease the Puda off the tavi and flip over to cook the other side. Pour a teaspoon of oil along the edge of the Puda so that the oil can go under the Puda to cook and brown the other side (about 1 minute).

When both sides are done, remove the Puda from the tavi and keep warm.

Make as many as required. Any left over batter can be kept in the refrigerator for a couple of days.

Bhagia

(vegetable fritters)

These are spicy snacks to be served with drinks. They are best eaten straightaway but they can be prepared ahead and served cold if wished. They're also good with ready-made mango chutney.

Serves: 6–8
Preparation time: 5–10 minutes
Cooking time: 30 minutes
Special equipment: wok/deep frying pan

Basic Bhagia Batter
225g (½ lb) gram flour (ground chick peas)
1 teaspoon salt
1 teaspoon chilli powder
1 tablespoon dhana (ground coriander)
1 teaspoon granulated sugar
2 tablespoons cooking oil
tepid water

oil for deep frying

Some suggested vegetables
Potato, sliced thinly
Onion, sliced thinly
Green pepper, sliced
Aubergine, thinly sliced
Mushrooms, whole or halved

Sift the flour into a bowl. Add the salt, chilli powder, dhana and sugar. Mix all the dry ingredients well. Add 2 tablespoons of cooking oil and rub into the flour with your fingertips. Add tepid water gradually, stirring the mixture continuously to avoid lumps forming. Add just enough water to make a thick pancake-type batter.

Heat the oil over medium heat. It should be ready for cooking when a little batter, dropped into the oil, sizzles and floats to the surface but does not brown immediately.

Take the prepared vegetables of your choice and dip a few pieces at a time into the batter and carefully drop them in the hot oil. Wait until all the pieces have come to the surface before turning them. Cook for 2–3 minutes, turning occasionally. Drain on absorbent paper towels.

Variation: Try this recipe with thickly sliced bananas instead of one of the suggested vegetables for a delicious alternative.

Tikhi Puree

(spicy puree) – see also plain puree (page 71)

These hot and spicy fried breads go very well served with a cup of Gujarati–style tea (see page 120) and some fried poppadums. They are also ideal to take on picnics.

Serves: 6–8
Preparation time: 25–30 minutes
Cooking time: 15–20 minutes
Special equipment: wok/deep frying pan

450g (1 lb) chapatti flour (ground wheat)
4 tablespoons cooking oil
3 cloves lasan (garlic)
4 mircha (green chillies)
1 teaspoon crushed jeera seeds (cumin)
1 teaspoon ground haldi (turmeric)
1½ teaspoons salt
warm water
oil for deep frying

Put the chapatti flour in a large bowl, add the oil and rub into the flour with the fingertips. Mince the lasan and mircha together and add to the flour with the crushed jeera, haldi and salt. Mix well, then add enough warm water to form a soft dough. (Wash hands thoroughly after handling mircha.)

Divide the dough into little balls the size of walnuts. Roll each ball out to a 7–8cm (3 inch) diameter round and spread the rolled discs on a clean tea towel.

Heat the oil over a medium heat. When a little piece of the dough is dropped into the oil and it rises to the surface almost immediately, the oil is ready for frying.

Lower a rolled out disc into the hot oil, wait until it rises to the surface then turn it over. Cook for 10–15 seconds or until lightly browned.

Remove from the oil and drain on absorbent paper towels. Repeat this process until all the purees are cooked.

Spicy Sweetcorn

This is my favourite snack dish because it is quick, easy and delicious. I like to serve it with some home made dahi (natural yoghurt) and Sev (see pages 85 and 94). Sev can also be bought ready made from many Indian grocery shops. This dish can be served very successfully as a first course at a dinner party.

Serves: 6
Preparation time: 2 minutes
Cooking time: 5–10 minutes

2 large cans sweetcorn (510g each)
6 tablespoons cooking oil
2 teaspoons rai (mustard seeds)

(contd. overleaf)

Spicy Sweetcorn (contd.)

2 teaspoons jeera seeds (cumin)
1 teaspoon ground haldi (turmeric)
3 cloves lasan (garlic)
3–4 mircha (green chillies)
6 heaped tablespoons dahi (natural yoghurt)
3 tablespoons chopped dhunia (green coriander)
Sev to serve (see below)

Open the cans of sweetcorn. Heat the oil in a heavy based pan. Add the rai and jeera seeds and cover the pan. Allow to 'pop' for a few seconds then add the contents of the cans, holding the lid ready to cover quickly. Be careful when you do this as the hot oil may splatter. Uncover the pan after a minute, reduce the heat to medium, add the haldi and mix well. Cook, uncovered for about 5 minutes or until nearly all the liquid has evaporated.

In the meantime, mince the mircha and the lasan together. Add to the pan and cook for a further minute. (Remember to wash your hands thoroughly after handling the mircha.) Stir in the dahi and chopped dhunia. Adjust the seasoning and serve in bowls sprinkled with a handful of sev.

Sev

(crispy gram flour snack)

Of all the dry snacks I suppose this must be one of the most popular because it is very versatile: it can be eaten as it is on its own, it can be mixed with other dry snacks to make different combinations, or it can be used to sprinkle over soft snack dishes to give them a crunch. An example of this is Spicy Sweetcorn (page 93). Sev is also used, crushed, in certain dishes to thicken and flavour them.

For this recipe you will need a snack-making device. It consists of a wide metal tube with a handle on one side and five or six discs that fit at the other end. Each of the discs has a different size and shape of holes cut into it. The disc with tiny round holes is used for sev making. The metal tube is filled with the sev batter and the handle is turned to squeeze the batter out of the holes straight into hot oil. If your chilli powder is coarse it may be a good idea to grind it down first before using it in this recipe. This is just to stop it from clogging up the holes in the disc.

Sev will stay fresh in an airtight container for up to a month.

Serves: (depends on use)
Preparation time: 7–10 minutes
Cooking time: 20–25 minutes
Special equipment: snack-maker
wok/deep frying pan

225g (½ lb) gram flour (ground chick peas)
1 teaspoon salt
1 teaspoon chilli powder
1 tablespoon cooking oil
1 tablespoon lemon juice
tepid water
oil for deep frying

Sift the flour and salt into a bowl. Sprinkle on the chilli powder and mix with a spoon. Make a hole in the centre and add the oil and lemon juice and rub in. Now add enough tepid water to make a very thick batter. It should have a slow dropping consistency. Fit the snack-maker with the correct disc and fill with some of the batter. Screw back the lid tightly and you are ready to start frying.

Pour cooking oil into a wok until it is 5–8cm (2–2½ inches) deep in the centre. Place it over medium heat and heat until a small drop of batter, when dropped into the oil, starts to sizzle almost immediately. This will mean that the oil has reached the correct temperature.

Holding the snack-maker tightly over the hot oil, turn the handle. Move your hands in a clockwise direction as the thin strands of batter enter the hot oil. Stop turning the handle when you have made between 1½–2 full circles in the oil and break off the strands.

Now put down the snack-maker and, using two slotted spoons, turn over the sev in the oil. Cook for 10–15 seconds then remove from the oil and drain on absorbent paper towels.

Sev should not be brown, so if your first batch is too brown you should reduce the heat slightly. If, on the other hand, it it still soft, you will need to turn up the heat before you cook your next batch. When all the sev is fried, allow to cool and then gently break up all the round nest shapes and pack in an airtight container. Use within 1 month.

Kachori

(stuffed patties)

These are little round dough parcels with a spicy savoury filling. They may be served with drinks or with a cup of Gujarati-style tea (see page 120) and some fried poppadums. They also make a wonderful first course. Simply lay two or three Kachori on a bed of shredded lettuce and pour over a little Green Coriander and Coconut Chutney (page 77). It is best to use fresh peas in this recipe.

Serves: 4–6
Preparation time: 7–10 minutes
Cooking time: 10 minutes
Special equipment: wok/deep frying pan

Filling
225g (½ lb) shelled peas
8 tablespoons cooking oil
1 teaspoon rai (mustard seeds)
1 teaspoon jeera seeds (cumin)
¼ teaspoon hing powder (asafoetida)
1–1½ teaspoons salt
1 teaspoon ground haldi (turmeric)
3–4 mircha (green chillies)
2 cloves lasan (garlic)
2 tablespoons desiccated coconut
1 tablespoon sesame seeds
juice of 1 lemon

Dough
125g (4 oz) plain flour
½ teaspoon salt
1 tablespoon cooking oil
tepid water

extra oil for frying

To make the filling: Wash and mince the peas. Heat the oil in a large non-stick frying pan. Add the rai and jeera seeds and allow to 'pop' with the lid on. Add the hing powder, the minced peas, salt and haldi. Mix well and cook for 5–7 minutes with the lid off.

Mince the mircha and the lasan together and add to the pan. Stir fry for 1 minute. Now add the desiccated coconut and the sesame seeds and continue to stir fry for another minute. (Wash your hands thoroughly after handling the mircha!)

Lastly, add the lemon juice and mix thoroughly. Adjust seasoning if required. Remove from heat and allow to cool completely.

To make the dough: Sift the flour and salt into a bowl.

Add the oil and rub in. Now add enough tepid water to form a soft dough.

Divide the dough into walnut sized balls. Roll a ball of dough out to a 8cm (3 inch) circle. Place a tablespoon of the filling in the centre and very carefully bring up the sides and press together at the top, enclosing the filling. Slightly flatten the shape and put aside. Repeat the process with the rest of the dough.

Now set the oil to heat over a low to medium heat. Do not allow the oil to get too hot. Lower a few kachoris into the oil and cook, turning occasionally until lightly browned all over. Drain on absorbent paper towels. Repeat until all the kachoris have been fried. Serve hot or cold.

Vegetable Samosas

These crispy triangular parcels are very popular among young and old alike. They can be served as bites at a drinks party or for the first course at a dinner party, in which case serve them on a bed of shredded lettuce with Green Coriander and Coconut Chutney to pour over (see page 77).

The stuffing is quite simple to make, but if you are new to Indian cookery you may find the thin pastry difficult. You can always cheat by using Chinese spring roll pastry. You will find this in Chinese food shops. It comes in a stack of frozen squares. To use, defrost at room temperature and gently separate the thin sheets of pastry and cut each in half, forming even rectangles. Chinese pastry will do the job but it is never as good as proper samosa pastry. I hope you will be brave and try making some.

Serves: 4–6
Preparation time: 30–40 minutes
Cooking time: 10–15 minutes
Special equipment: wok/deep frying pan

Filling
1 large onion
1 large potato
3 carrots
100g (4 oz) frozen peas
8 tablespoons cooking oil
1 teaspoon rai (mustard seeds)
1 teaspoon jeera seeds (cumin)
1½ teaspoons ground haldi (turmeric)
1½ teaspoons salt
1 teaspoon chilli powder
2 tablespoons dhana (ground coriander)
1 teaspoon granulated sugar
2 tablespoons sesame seeds
juice of 1 lemon

Pastry
500g (1 lb) plain flour
1 teaspoon salt
1 teaspoon oil
1 teaspoon lemon juice
cold water
plain flour, in a dredger
10–12 tablespoons oil for brushing
oil for deep frying

First make the filling: Peel and chop the onion finely. Peel the potato and carrots and cut into 1cm (½ inch) cubes and keep all the vegetables separate. Defrost the peas at room temperature.

Heat the oil in a large frying pan, add the rai and jeera

seeds and cover the pan for a few seconds until the 'popping' has stopped. Carefully add the onion, and quickly cover again to avoid splattering. After a few seconds uncover the pan and stir the onion. Lower the heat to medium and cook for 1 minute. Then add the carrots, stir and cover the pan. Cook for a further 2–3 minutes.

Now add the potato, haldi and salt. Mix well and cook, covered, for a further 2 minutes. Uncover the pan, add the peas and continue cooking until all the vegetables are tender. Add the chilli powder, dhana and sugar. Cook for a further 2 minutes.

Lastly, mix in the sesame seeds and lemon juice and cook for a minute longer. Remove from heat and allow to cool.

Meanwhile, make the pastry: Sift the flour and salt into a bowl. Rub in the oil and lemon juice and add enough cold water to bind into a soft pliable dough. Divide the dough into walnut sized pieces. Flatten each piece between the palms of your hands and roll out on a floured board to approximately 7–8cm (3 inch) in diameter.

Do this with the rest of the dough, spreading them all out on a clean tray or work surface. Brush oil liberally over all the dough discs and sprinkle with the flour from the flour dredger. Pair up the discs with the oiled and floured sides facing.

Now set your tavi or non-stick frying pan over low heat. Roll out each pair of discs carefully on a floured board taking care not to allow the dough to pleat as you roll. Roll as thin as you can keeping the round shape.

Cook on a heated tavi or frying pan, turning quickly as soon as little bubbles are seen to appear. Separate out the 2 layers carefully and stack with the spotted sides down. This operation takes literally seconds. It is very important not to over cook the pastry at this stage as it will be cooked again later. Wrap them in a clean tea towel as you cook them to keep them soft.

When all the pastry is cooked in this way re-stack them on a chopping board, making a neat pile. Now trim off the 2 opposite edges of the pastry stack, as shown in the diagram, leaving something resembling a square. Make another cut in the centre making 2 stacks of long strips. The trimmed off edges can be fried and served with drinks.

Adjust the seasoning in the now cold filling and fill the samosas as follows. First make a paste of flour and water to stick the pastry envelopes down (1 tablespoon plain flour and 1 tablespoon water). Taking a strip of pastry with the long edge to your right, fold along line AB. Brush the paste along the edge B to C and bring A to meet C. Press down to stick. Fill the resulting envelope with some of the filling and wrap the flap over and secure with more paste.

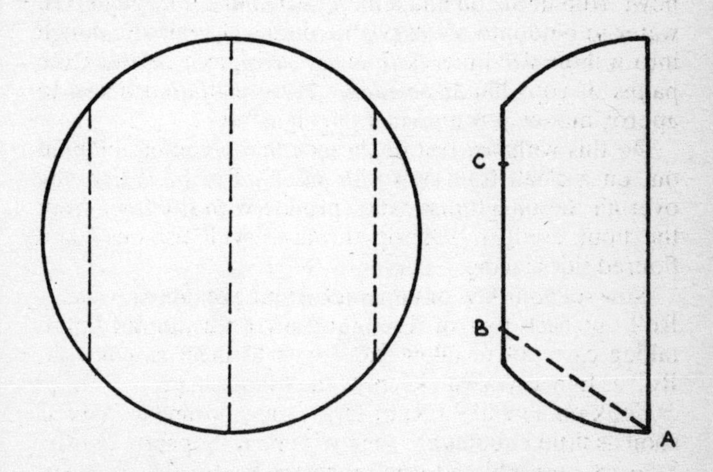

Folding a samosa.

Make all the samosas in this way and spread out on a tray until ready to fry. Deep fry at medium heat until crisp and golden. Drain on absorbent paper towels. Samosas can be served either hot or cold.

Masala Dhosa

(stuffed pancakes)

This is a good dish for a dinner party and it will be easy to double the quantities given here if you wish to serve a larger number of people. Alternatively, you might like to double the quantity and freeze the left over batter, after proving for 24 hours, so that you have some in store. Do make sure you use a large bowl to mix the batter ingredients and leave it in a warm place, but not too hot, as it may froth and spill over if the bowl is too small or the temperature is too high. To use the frozen batter, just defrost at room temperature for 4–5 hours and then follow the recipe for making the pancakes. It is not advisable to freeze the filling, so make fresh filling when it is needed.

To make a delicious supper or a first course at a dinner party, serve these covered with Sambhar and a tablespoon of Spicy Yoghurt Chutney (see pages 105 and 79).

Serves: 6–8
Preparation time: 24 hours
Cooking time: 15–20 minutes

Dhosa Batter

450g (2 cups) rice flour
115g (½ cup) urid flour (ground black beans)
½ teaspoon salt
1 tablespoon dahi (natural yoghurt)
warm water

Filling
1 large potato
1 large onion
2 tablespoons oil
½ teaspoon rai (mustard seeds)
½ teaspoon jeera seeds (cumin)
1 teaspoon salt
½ teaspoon ground haldi (turmeric)
½ teaspoon chilli powder
1 tablespoon dhana (ground coriander)
½ teaspoon granulated sugar

oil for making dhosas

Mix the batter ingredients together using enough warm water to make a porridge-like consistency, cover and leave in a warm place for 24 hours.

To make the filling: peel and chop both the potato and onion coarsely, but keep them separate. Heat the oil in a frying pan, add the rai and jeera seeds and cover the pan. When they have stopped 'popping', add the potato, salt and haldi. Mix well, reduce heat and cook, covered, for 5 minutes. Add the onion, chilli powder, dhana and sugar, mix thoroughly and cook with the lid on for a further 10 minutes, stirring occasionally.

To make the dhosa: heat 1 tablespoon of oil in a frying pan (preferably non-stick) over medium to high heat. Pour a ladleful of the batter into the middle and tip the frying pan from side to side in order to spread the batter. Cook for 1 minute and then turn over using a spatula and cook the other side for 30 seconds. Turn out onto a serving plate, put some filling in the middle and fold like a pancake.

Idli

(steamed rice cakes)

Idli originates from the south of India where people are poor and cannot afford to eat the highly priced rice grain, so instead they use rice flour made from inferior quality rice and make steamed rice cakes from it. These are worth trying.

For this recipe you will need a double steamer and an Idli stand. An Idli stand is a three tiered utensil with four hollows in each tier, a little like a bun tin. The Idli batter is poured into each hollow (as you would with Yorkshire Pudding batter) and then the whole stand is put inside the double steamer to cook the Idli.

If you wish to buy an Idli stand there are some shops that specialize in utensils used for Indian cookery, but, of course, it is always possible to improvise. If you have a shallow metal tray or dish that will fit comfortably in the steamer, then you can use it to cook your Idli in. When cooked, cut into diamond shapes and ease out of the tray or dish with a flat implement. Serve in deep plates or bowls with a ladleful of Sambhar poured over (see opposite). Lastly, spoon some Spicy Yoghurt Chutney (page 79) over the Sambhar for a final touch.

This is a wonderful dinner party dish with a difference.

Serves: 8
Preparation time: 24 hours
Cooking time: 30 minutes
Special equipment: double steamer
Idli stand

775g (3 cups) rice flour
225g (1 cup) urid flour (ground black beans)
1½ teaspoons salt
4 tablespoons oil

warm water
Eno's fruit salt (available from most Chemists)

Put the two different flours with the salt and oil in a glass bowl. Add enough warm water to make a thick porridge-like consistency. Cover and leave in a warm place for 24 hours.

Put some water in the bottom of a double steamer and bring to the boil. If you do not have an Idli stand a metal tin that fits into the steamer will do. Oil well.

Take 2 ladlefuls of the batter in a bowl and add 1 teaspoon of Eno's fruit salt. Quickly mix and fill the Idli tins or whatever is being used. The batter will spread and take the shape of the container. Steam for 10 minutes. Remove and keep warm. Use up all the batter using 1 teaspoon of Eno's fruit salt with each batch.

If Idli is cooked in a tin, cut into diamond shapes before serving.

Sambhar
(dall with vegetables)

This recipe is different in the way pulses and vegetables come together in one dish. It is normally served with Idli (above) or Masala Dhosa (see page 102) but can also be served with rice. Reduce it by boiling to a thick soup-like consistency and serve in a gravy boat to pour over your Idli or Masala Dhosa as desired. This is originally a South Indian dish but is very popular all over India.

Serves: 4–6
Preparation time: 10–15 minutes
Cooking time: 2 hours
Special equipment: pressure cooker

175g (6 oz) toor dall (split pigeon peas)
1.5 litres (3 pints) water
50g (2 oz) frozen peas
1 small potato, cubed
1 small carrot, cubed
1 small onion, sliced
1 small aubergine, chopped
4–5 florets of cauliflower
water for boiling
8 tablespoons cooking oil
1 teaspoon rai (mustard seeds)
1 teaspoon jeera seeds (cumin)
pinch hing powder (asafoetida)
2 teaspoons salt
1½ teaspoons ground haldi (turmeric)
2.5cm (1 inch) adrak (root ginger)
3 cloves lasan (garlic)
1 small can tomatoes (230g)
2.5cm (1 inch) tuj (cinnamon stick)
4 lavang (cloves)
3 tablespoons dhana (ground coriander)
1½ teaspoons chilli powder
small piece amli (tamarind), soaked in boiling water
2 tablespoons gor (jaggery) or brown sugar
juice of 1 lemon
5 limdi (curry leaves)

Boil the toor dall for 1 hour in the water or pressure cook for 20 minutes at high pressure, whisk and allow to simmer. In another pan boil all the vegetables (except the canned tomatoes) in some water for 10 minutes and drain.

Heat 4 tablespoons of the oil, add the rai and jeera seeds, cover and allow to ‘pop’, then add a pinch of hing powder and immediately add all the cooked vegetables. Add the salt and haldi and mix well. Mince the adrak, lasan and tomatoes, and add to the vegetables. Simmer the vegetable mixture for 5 minutes and then add to the cooked toor dall.

Heat the remaining 4 tablespoons of oil, add the tuj, lavang, dhana and chilli powder and stir fry for 1 minute. Add to the toor dall and continue to simmer for another 10 minutes.

Strain all the juice out of the amli and add to the dall with the gor, lemon juice and limdi. Taste and adjust seasoning. Simmer for another 30 minutes.

9

SWEETS, DESSERTS AND OTHER THINGS

In India sweet dishes are served as part of the main meal. Spicy vegetable dishes and breads such as puree (page 71) are served with the sweet dish as the first course of a meal followed by a rice and pulse dish for the main course. A dessert as such is not served. Most people prefer to end their meal with fresh fruit.

Indian sweet dishes tend to be quite rich in the use of milk and ghee so they should be served in small quantities. Little glass bowls are ideal for this.

Whether you would like to do what the Indians do or decide to have your sweet dish at the end of a meal, I am sure you will enjoy the recipes in this section of the book.

Try them and you will see that they are not difficult at all.

A number of these recipes use almonds which will need peeling. The quickest way to do this is to steep them in hot water for 10 minutes. This loosens the skins and makes it easier to peel them.

Shrikhand

(sweetened curd cheese)

This is one of those sweet dishes that is served alongside savoury dishes as the first course of a meal. Serve Puree (page 71) with this dish and sprinkle with the almonds, pistachios and elchi just before serving. Unused Shrikhand will keep in the refrigerator for up to one week.

Serves: 6
Preparation time: 1 hour
Cooking time: nil

450g (1 lb) curd cheese
1 tablespoon dahi (natural yoghurt)
450g (1 lb) caster sugar
few strands of kessar (saffron), soaked in:
1 tablespoon milk
100g (4 oz) almonds (blanched and sliced)
50g (2 oz) pistachios (chopped)
1 teaspoon ground elchi seeds (cardamom)

Whisk the curd cheese, dahi and sugar together. Cover and leave for 1 hour for the sugar to dissolve. Whisk again, add the milk with the kessar in and mix well.

Place in the refrigerator and serve cold, sprinkled with the almonds, pistachios and elchi.

Gulab Jamuns

For this recipe to succeed make sure the syrup is right before you start frying your little balls of dough. When testing the syrup, allow to cool a little before touching it with your fingers as hot sugar will burn.

Serve these for dessert with a little of the syrup or with some ready made vanilla ice cream. Keeps well in a refrigerator for up to one week.

Serves: 8–10
Preparation time: 10–15 minutes
Cooking time: 20–30 minutes
Special equipment: wok/deep frying pan

Syrup
425ml (1½ cups) water
350g (2 cups) granulated sugar

Dough
225g (2 cups) powdered milk
50g (½ cup) plain flour
¼ teaspoon bicarbonate of soda
1 teaspoon ground elchi seeds (cardamom)
1 teaspoon ghee, melted
milk at room temperature

oil for frying (approximately 1.5 litres/3 pints)

To make sugar syrup, combine the water and sugar in a pan and bring to the boil slowly. Increase heat and boil rapidly for 5 minutes. Test if the syrup is the right consistency by taking a teaspoon of the syrup, allowing it to cool and then, between thumb and forefinger, pulling it to see if a 'string' forms. If the syrup is not ready, continue to boil and test at minute intervals. When ready, remove from heat but keep warm.

Sieve the powdered milk, flour and bicarbonate of soda several times to incorporate air. Add the elchi and rub in the ghee very lightly. It is essential to be light with your fingers. Use enough milk to bind the mixture into a soft ball. Do not knead. Still being very gentle, divide into grape sized balls and fry in medium hot oil until golden. Drain and throw straight into the hot syrup.

When all the Gulab Jamuns are in the syrup, allow to cool completely. Empty into a glass bowl and refrigerate.

Gulab Jamuns Rolled in Coconut

When mixing the ingredients together, do it very gently with a fork. Finally go in with your hands and very gently form little sausage shapes just before frying. These are ideal to serve at dinner parties as they can be made 2 or 3 days in advance. I like to serve them with a scoop of ready made vanilla ice cream.

Serves: 8–10
Preparation time: 10 minutes
Cooking time: 20–30 minutes
Special equipment: wok/deep frying pan

Syrup
350g (2 cups) granulated sugar
285ml (1 cup) water

Dough
1 can unsweetened condensed milk (379g)
200g (2½ cups) plain flour
50g (½ cup) semolina
3 teaspoons baking powder
150ml (½ cup) ghee

(contd. overleaf)

Gulab Jamuns Rolled in Coconut (contd.)

150ml (½ cup) dahi (natural yoghurt)
4 teaspoons rose water
2 tablespoons chopped almonds
1 teaspoon ground elchi seeds (cardamom)
1 tablespoon chopped pistachios
a few strands of kessar (saffron)
50g (½ cup) desiccated coconut

oil for frying (approx. 1.5 litres/3 pints)

Make the syrup as in the previous recipe but the consistency must be thicker, similar to that of honey.

Combine all the other ingredients except the desiccated coconut. Shape the Jamuns into sausage shapes and deep fry until golden brown.

Soak in the hot syrup for a few minutes, drain and roll in the coconut.

Cool completely then put in the fridge.

Basudi
(milk pudding)

Basudi is served with Puree (page 71) as the first course of a meal with a vegetable dish as an accompaniment. It is served in small quantities as it can be very filling, and as a general rule it is served only at special occasions and dinner parties. It is a good idea to use a large heavy based pan for this to prevent the milk boiling over. Stir often and on no account leave it for any length of time. It can easily burn and stick to the bottom of the pan.

Serves: 4–6
Preparation time: 10 minutes
Cooking time: 1–1½ hours

1 litre (2 pints) full cream milk
4 tablespoons granulated sugar
1 teaspoon ground elchi seeds (cardamom)
1 tablespoon almonds, peeled and sliced
1 tablespoon pistachios, sliced

Bring the milk to the boil and simmer, stirring occasionally until thick and creamy. You should end up with approximately 375ml (¾ pint) of thickened milk.

Remove from the heat, add the sugar, ground elchi, sliced almonds and pistachios and stir until the sugar has dissolved. Allow to cool, stirring occasionally to avoid a skin forming on the surface.

Empty into a serving dish and refrigerate until required.

Basudi with Fruit
(milk pudding with fruit)

This is a much lighter sweet dish and it is served either as part of the first course or on its own for dessert. It is an attractive looking dish and may be served quite successfully at a dinner party. It is important to stir often while it is cooling to avoid skin forming on the surface.

Serves: 6–8
Preparation time: 10 minutes
Cooking time: 15 minutes

½ tablespoon custard powder
1 litre (2 pints) full cream milk
6 tablespoons granulated sugar
1 teaspoon ground elchi seeds (cardamom)
2 tablespoons almonds, peeled and sliced
1 medium can mixed fruit (420g)

Mix the custard powder with a little of the milk in a small bowl and keep to one side. Bring the rest of the milk to the boil and simmer for 15 minutes.

Add the custard powder paste, stir and remove from heat. Now add the sugar, elchi seeds and almonds and allow to cool completely, stirring occasionally to avoid a skin forming on the surface.

When quite cold, strain the liquid out of the mixed fruit and add the fruit to the pan. Stir and empty into a serving dish and keep refrigerated until ready to serve.

Dudh Paak

(rice pudding)

This is rice pudding with a difference. It is well worth trying. The rice soaks up the milk as it cooks and becomes plump while the milk thickens. It all ends up in a thick creamy pudding which is flavoured with exotic spices.

Serves: 4–6
Preparation time: 5–7 minutes
Cooking time: 40–50 minutes

75g (½ cup) long grain rice
1 litre (2 pints) full fat milk
1 teaspoon ghee (page 84)
4 tablespoons granulated sugar
1 teaspoon ground elchi seeds (cardamom)
1 tablespoon almonds, peeled and sliced
1 tablespoon pistachios, sliced
½ teaspoon grated jaiphal (nutmeg)

Wash the rice and soak for 5 minutes. Bring the milk to the boil in a large heavy based pan. When boiling, add the strained rice and the ghee and bring back to the boil. Reduce the heat and simmer, stirring occasionally, until the mixture is quite thick. It should have reduced to half the original quantity. Remove from heat.

Now add the sugar, ground elchi, sliced almonds, sliced pistachios and grated jaiphal. Cool completely, stirring often to avoid skin forming on the surface of the pudding.

Pour into a serving dish and refrigerate for a few hours before serving.

Sweet Sev

This is a wonderful way of serving sev. If you are serving it to guests you may wish to make it ahead and keep it warm in a moderately cool oven (300F/150C/Gas mark 2), or you may leave your guests to chat while you go away and cook it. The smell of the vermicelli stir frying in the ghee will make their mouths water with anticipation!

Serves: 4
Preparation time: nil
Cooking time: 10–15 minutes

2 tablespoons ghee (page 84)
125g (1 cup) broken sev (page 94)
600ml (2 cups) boiling water
115g (½ cup) granulated sugar
¼ teaspoon ground elchi seeds (cardamom)

Heat the ghee in a heavy based pan. Add the sev and stir fry for 2–3 minutes, or until crisp and brown.

Add the boiling water, reduce the heat to medium, cover and cook for 5–7 minutes. Stir occasionally during this time.

Add the sugar and elchi, stir well and simmer for 1 minute. Serve hot.

Lapsi
(crushed wheat)

Like most Indian sweet dishes, this is served along with the savoury dishes as the first course. The smell in the kitchen is quite amazing when Lapsi is being cooked. It is important to keep the Lapsi moving all the time while stir frying.

Serves: 6–8
Preparation time: 10–15 minutes
Cooking time: 1¼ hours

150ml (½ cup) ghee (page 84)
100g (1 cup) lapsi (crushed wheat)
4 lavang (cloves)
2 × 2.5cm (1 inch) pieces of tuj (cinnamon stick)
1 litre (4 cups) boiling water
225g (1 cup) granulated sugar
½ teaspoon crushed elchi seeds (cardamom)
1 tablespoon almonds, peeled and sliced

Heat the ghee in a heavy based pan. Add the lapsi, lavang and tuj. Reduce the heat to medium and cook, stirring all the time, until evenly brown (about 3–5 minutes). Then add the boiling water, cover the pan and simmer for up to 30 minutes. Stir occasionally during this time. Meanwhile, pre-heat the oven to 350F/180C/Gas mark 4.

Test a grain of lapsi between thumb and forefinger. It should feel soft and not grainy. Allow more cooking time if required. You may also have to add a little more water.

When lapsi is properly cooked, add the sugar and the crushed elchi. Mix well and empty into an ovenproof dish. Cover the dish and put in the oven.

After about 7 minutes, reduce the heat to 200F/100C/Gas mark low and cook for 15 minutes. Stir in the sliced almonds and cook for a further 10 minutes. Serve hot.

Seero
(semolina pudding)

Seero is one of my favourites. I always make plenty because it heats up beautifully in a microwave oven or a conventional one. You can either serve it for the first course at a dinner party, along with vegetable and pulse dishes, or on its own at the end for dessert.

Serves: 6–8
Preparation time: 10–15 minutes
Cooking time: 15–20 minutes

600ml (1 pint) milk
3 tablespoons ghee (page 84)
225g (½ lb) semolina
225g (½ lb) granulated sugar
½ teaspoon ground elchi seeds (cardamom)
1 tablespoon almonds, peeled and roughly chopped

Bring the milk to the boil and keep to one side.

Heat the ghee in a heavy based pan, add the semolina and stir fry over medium heat until slightly browned (about 5 minutes).

Pour the hot milk in, stirring all the time. Lower the heat, cover the pan and cook for 5 minutes. Give it a good stir now and again. Cook, covered, for another 2–3 minutes. Remove from heat and mix in the elchi and the almonds.

Leave covered until ready to serve. Serve hot.

Vedmi

(sweet stuffed chapattis)

Even though these are more time consuming than many of the other sweet dishes they are well worth the time and trouble. If you do not have a microwave oven, put the cooked, drained toor dall in a large deep pan with the sugar and cook, stirring all the time until thickened. Take care when you do this as the mixture in the pan is very hot and will tend to splutter as it thickens.

Serves: 4–6
Preparation time: 30 minutes
Cooking time: 50–60 minutes
Special equipment: pressure cooker
microwave oven (although not essential)

225g (½ lb) toor dall (split pigeon peas)
1 litre (2 pints) hot water
225g (½ lb) granulated sugar
1 teaspoon ground elchi seeds (cardamom)
½ teaspoon grated jaiphal (nutmeg)
½ teaspoon ground lavang (cloves)
450g (2 cups) chapatti flour (ground wheat)
1 tablespoon cooking oil
hot water

oil for shallow frying
melted ghee for serving

Wash the toor dall and soak in hot water for 30 minutes. Strain and place in a pressure cooker with hot water to cover the dall by about 2.5cm (1 inch). Pressure cook for

15–20 minutes at medium pressure. Remove from the heat and leave for 30 minutes before opening the pressure cooker. The dall should be soft and pulpy. If it is still hard, cook for a few more minutes.

When cooked do not stir but drain off as much water as possible and then empty into a large glass bowl. Add the sugar and mix well. Cover the bowl with a plate and cook in the microwave oven at full power for 5 minutes. It should end up with a dry, dough-like consistency. If it is still too wet, give it more time in the microwave until the right consistency is reached. Allow to cool completely. Mix in the elchi, jaiphal and lavang. Form into large walnut sized balls.

In another bowl, take the chapatti flour and make a hole in the middle. Put in the oil and gradually add enough hot water to form a soft dough.

Make slightly smaller balls from this dough. Roll out each ball into approximately 5cm (2 inch) circles. Place a ball of dall in the centre and bring up the sides of the dough and press together at the top enclosing the ball of dall completely. Gently flatten between the palms and dip in some flour. Roll out very carefully to a thick round shape about 7–10cm (3–4 inches) in diameter.

Heat a tavi or frying pan over gentle heat. Place the Vedmi on the tavi or frying pan and cook on both sides for approximately 1 minute each side. (Very gentle handling will be necessary at this stage.) Lastly, trickle a teaspoon of oil around the Vedmi and cook for another 30 seconds each side. Serve hot.

It is much easier to cook all the Vedmi dry on the tavi first and then cook again with a little oil only when required. Pour over a tablespoon of melted ghee just before serving.

Gujarati-style Tea

Feel the warm glow down your throat as you sip this delicious warming tea on a cold winter's day. The Tea Masala is optional but it is well worth trying (see below). This tea can also be used to help soothe the throat when you are suffering from a cold.

Serves: 2
Preparation time: 2 minutes
Cooking time: 4–5 minutes

425ml (1½ cups) water
1cm (½ inch) adrak, grated (root ginger)
4 teaspoons granulated sugar
5–6 phoodino leaves (mint)
¼ teaspoon tea masala (see below) – optional
2 teaspoons tea leaves (any brand)
285ml (1 cup) full fat milk

Boil the water with the grated adrak in a small saucepan for 1 minute. Add the sugar, mint, tea masala and the tea leaves.

Boil for another minute. Now add the milk and bring to the boil. Simmer for 1 minute then strain into tea cups and serve.

Tea Masala

Preparation time: 5 minutes
Cooking time: nil
Special equipment: coffee grinder

120g (4 oz) white peppercorns
90g (3 oz) dried root ginger
60g (2 oz) tuj (cinnamon stick)
28g (1 oz) elchi seeds (cardamom)
25 lavang (cloves)

Grind all the ingredients together in a coffee grinder and store in an airtight container. Tea masala will keep indefinitely if stored in this way.

Ukaro

(hot spicy milk drink)

This is a warming drink, best drunk at bedtime. Do watch over this as it has a tendency to boil over.

Serves: 2
Preparation time: 2 minutes
Cooking time: 5–10 minutes

285ml (1 cup) water
2.5cm (1 inch) adrak, grated (root ginger)
3–4 phoodino leaves (mint) – optional
¼ teaspoon tea masala
4 teaspoons granulated sugar
570ml (2 cups) full fat milk

Put the water and adrak together in a milk pan and bring to the boil. Simmer for 1 minute, then add the phoodino leaves, tea masala and the sugar. Simmer for a further minute.

Now add the milk and bring back to the boil. Simmer for 1 more minute and strain into 2 tea cups.

Lassi

(yoghurt drink)

Lassi is supposed to cool the blood and in India it is given to farm workers for this reason. It keeps up to 3 days in a refrigerator and I always like to have a jugful in the fridge during the summer months. This is a yoghurt drink with a difference. I do hope you will try it. The dahi in this recipe may be bought or home made (see page 85).

Serves: 3–4
Preparation time: 3–5 minutes plus chilling time
Cooking time: nil

500ml (1 pint) dahi (natural yoghurt)
500ml (1 pint) cold water
2 teaspoons crushed jeera seeds (cumin)
2 teaspoons salt (or to taste)
2 tablespoons finely chopped dhunia (green coriander)

Empty the dahi into a large glass bowl. Add the water, salt and the crushed jeera and whisk until frothy. Salt to taste.

Pour into a glass jug and refrigerate for a few hours before serving. Serve cold in tall glasses with a cube of ice and a little chopped dhunia.

Variation: Serve with finely chopped phoodino (mint) instead of the dhunia.

Garam Masala

This mixture of spices is available from most Indian grocery shops but here is a recipe for those of you who wish to make your own. Use this mixture very sparingly sprinkled over curries.

Preparation time: 10 minutes
Cooking time: 30 minutes
Special equipment: coffee grinder

225g (8 oz) dhana seeds (coriander)
125g (4 oz) jeera seeds (cumin)
125g (4 oz) elchi seeds (cardamom)
50g (2 oz) tuj (cinnamon sticks)
125g (4 oz) kala mari (black peppercorns)
50g (2 oz) lavang (cloves)
1 teaspoon grated jaiphal (nutmeg)

Preheat the oven to 300F/150C/Gas mark 2 and roast the dhana and jeera seeds separately, stirring occasionally for half an hour.

Allow to cool then grind each ingredient separately until very fine. Mix thoroughly and pack in an air-tight container until needed.

Will store for up to a year if kept air-tight.

INDEX

MORE PAPERFRONT COOKBOOKS

Each uniform with this book

THE CURRY SECRET

The curry book with a difference! It reveals the secret of *Indian Restaurant Cooking* – that particularly interesting and distinctive variety that is served in Indian restaurants all over the world. Kris Dhillon reveals all and offers you the opportunity to reproduce that elusive taste in your own kitchen.

AN INDIAN HOUSEWIFE'S RECIPE BOOK

Laxmi Khurana demolishes the myth that Indian cookery is cumbersome and time-consuming. She presents simple and economical family recipes made from ingredients and spices which are widely available. Not only are curries included; so is an array of starters, snacks, raitas, chutneys, pickles and sweets. Everything, in fact, that characterises Indian cookery for people all over the world.

THE STIR FRY COOK

Packed with recipes that are quick and simple, needing the minimum of preparation, equipment and washing-up! Caroline Young shows how easy it is to create meals all in one pan in less than 30 minutes with the aid of a good frying pan or wok.

OUR PUBLISHING POLICY

HOW WE CHOOSE

Our policy is to consider every deserving manuscript and we can give special editorial help where an author is an authority on his subject but an inexperienced writer. We are rigorously selective in the choice of books we publish. We set the highest standards of editorial quality and accuracy. This means that a *Paperfront* is easy to understand and delightful to read. Where illustrations are necessary to convey points of detail, these are drawn up by a subject specialist artist from our panel.

HOW WE KEEP PRICES LOW

We aim for the big seller. This enables us to order enormous print runs and achieve the lowest price for you. Unfortunately, this means that you will not find in the *Paperfront* list any titles on obscure subjects of minority interest only. These could not be printed in large enough quantities to be sold for the low price at which we offer this series.

We sell almost all our *Paperfronts* at the same unit price. This saves a lot of fiddling about in our clerical departments and helps us to give you world-beating value. Under this system, the longer titles are offered at a price which we believe to be unmatched by any publisher in the world.

OUR DISTRIBUTION SYSTEM

Because of the competitive price, and the rapid turnover, *Paperfronts* are possibly the most profitable line a bookseller can handle. They are stocked by the best bookshops all over the world. It may be that your bookseller has run out of stock of a particular title. If so, he can order more from us at any time—we have a fine reputation for "same day" despatch, and we supply any order, however small (even a single copy), to any bookseller who has an account with us. We prefer you to buy from your bookseller, as this reminds him of the strong underlying public demand for *Paperfronts.* Members of the public who live in remote places, or who are housebound, or whose local bookseller is unco-operative, can order direct from us by post.

FREE

If you would like an up-to-date list of all *Paperfront* titles currently available, send a stamped self-addressed envelope to
ELLIOT RIGHT WAY BOOKS, BRIGHTON RD.,
LOWER KINGSWOOD, SURREY, KT20 6TD, U.K.